Pagan Portals
Reclaiming Witchcraft

Pagan Portals
Reclaiming Witchcraft

Irisanya Moon

MOON
BOOKS

Winchester, UK
Washington, USA

JOHN HUNT PUBLISHING

First published by Moon Books, 2020
Moon Books is an imprint of John Hunt Publishing Ltd., No. 3 East Street, Alresford
Hampshire SO24 9EE, UK
office@jhpbooks.net
www.johnhuntpublishing.com
www.moon-books.net

For distributor details and how to order please visit the 'Ordering' section on our website.

Text copyright: Irisanya Moon 2019

ISBN: 978 1 78904 212 2
978 1 78904 213 9 (ebook)
Library of Congress Control Number: 2019943768

A CIP catalogue record for this book is available from the British Library.

Design: Stuart Davies

UK: Printed and bound by CPI Group (UK) Ltd, Croydon, CR0 4YY
US: Printed and bound by Thomson-Shore, 7300 West Joy Road, Dexter, MI 48130

We operate a distinctive and ethical publishing philosophy in
all areas of our business, from our global network of authors to
production and worldwide distribution.

Contents

Acknowledgements   vi
Introduction   1
A Welcome   3
Magickal Beginning   5

Chapter 1: The Beginning / History   7
Chapter 2: Principles of Unity / Beliefs   11
Chapter 3: Groups & Structures   16
Chapter 4: Your Own Spiritual Authority / How to Practice   25
Chapter 5: Ritual   33
Chapter 6: Core Classes   49
Chapter 7: Witchcamps around the World   66
Chapter 8: Across the Generations   73
Chapter 9: Magickal Activism   77

Conclusion   85
Appendix A: Ritual Planning & Outline   87
Appendix B: Resources   91

Acknowledgements

I want to acknowledge my lineage in Reclaiming and the people from whom I have learned and grown, mostly from mistakes and missteps, and all the trappings of this human experience.

I started my Reclaiming community experience by attending California Witchcamp as recommended by Sefora and organized by Madrone, and took my first path/class with Rose May Dance and John Brazaitis.

I proceeded to take Elements of Magick, Rites of Passages, Iron Pentacle, Pearl Pentacle, and a year-long Priestess Journey with Copper Persephone and Diana Melisabee. I continued in a Priestess Apprenticeship with Ravyn Stanfield, Suzanne Sterling and Dawn Isidora. I was initiated into the Reclaiming tradition in 2014.

I've been in ritual planning cells with Copper Persephone, Diana Melisabee, Mer, Ross, Helen Hawk, Pavini, Phoenix Le Fae, Dailey, Gwion, Justin, Root, Norma, Bran, Susan, Lizann, Bran, Vixen, Yule, Coyote, Honeycomb, Neon Animal, Lilith, Bryan, and probably others. (Forgive me!)

I've taught with a myriad of folx, including Copper, Urania, Riyana, Laura M., Georgie, Cypress, Inanna, Gwion, Justin, Phoenix, Heidi, Honeycomb, Lore, Ewa, Root, Rose May Dance, Pandora, Willow Kelly, River Roberts, Shiray, Sharon J., Sue D., Linda B., Tracey C., George F., Rock, Vesper, Hilary, Mykel, K-Mo, Sequoia, Jessica Dreamer, Elinor P., and likely others.

And I thank the magick and work of M. Macha Nightmare, Anne Hill, Deborah Oak, Donald L. Engstrom-Reese, T Thorn Coyle, Jane Meredith. Gede Parma (Fio), and more.

I am ever thankful to Starhawk and those who came before for calling out to me before I knew Reclaiming was a real group of people and not just a book called 'Spiral Dance' I am grateful to the godds who walk with me and nudge me in directions I didn't expect to travel.

I'm grateful to those who have gone before me, those who paved roads and worked magick I can feel in my bones. I thank those whose names I know and those whose names I have yet to uncover. Raven Moonshadow, Luanne, Judy Foster, Moher Downing, Tyrell O'Neal, Angela Magara, Beth Bone Blossom, Victor and Cora Anderson, Rebecca Tidewalker, Margot Adler, Gwydion Pendderwen, Lizann Bassham, and so many others.

I am thankful to Trevor and the Moon Books community for their support and encouragement.

And I am thankful to my partner who has been very patient as I spend hours writing in my office.

Introduction

The story of Reclaiming is still emerging. To say that this is a definitive work would be not only incorrect, but also stifling. I've been a part of the tradition since 1998, but only in active community leadership since 2009. Even in that timeframe, I have seen Reclaiming shift and adjust and expand to be more inclusive and representative of its community members.

This is not to say we don't have room to grow even more, to learn more, and to be more aware of our collective and personal shadows. Reclaiming is not a perfect tradition as we are made up of perfectly imperfect humans.

When I was approached to write this book, I was nervous about representing and describing the tradition that has held me so gently. How do you talk about a place that feels like home? How do you express the magick and the love? How do you describe the ecstasy?

The truth is, you can't. I can't bring you into a ritual with just words. I can't tell you how your heart feels when you see people who have your back and who have held your hand as you cried away the old stories. I can't tell you what it's like to be in meetings and camps and initiations. I can't tell you about sitting at a picnic table, listening to an elder laugh, and have you realize what a powerful moment it was.

Here's what I can do. I can tell you what Reclaiming is, how it is arranged, and what it strives to do. I can tell you that we work hard to better understand ourselves and become more resilient in the ever-shifting landscape of power. I can tell you that we're committed to dismantling structures of oppression, both those outside and inside our bodies.

I can tell you that we have our challenges and our worries. I can tell you that we sometimes trip over our egos and hurt each other. I can tell you that we sometimes gossip and sometimes mean exactly what we say.

I can tell you that group dynamics are real and we're not always at our best. But, most of the time, we think well of each other. Much of the time, we know how to take a deep breath so we don't say more than we need to say. Much of the time, we are able to hear feedback and take a closer look at a mistake.

We are a living, growing, ecstatic, and learning tradition. I learned what Reclaiming was from a book: 'The Spiral Dance' by Starhawk. But I learned what Reclaiming really was by going to classes and camps, attending and planning rituals, and sitting in meeting after meeting.

And I didn't write this book for those who are already in Reclaiming. I wrote it for the person who has heard the 'rumors' and wants to know the reality - at least my version of it.

I am fully aware that this is my version of Reclaiming, and I hope that my vast experience in the tradition as a student, teacher, Witchcamp teacher, initiate, initiator, ritual planner, cell member, organizer, and team leader helps this conversation.

I am fully aware that there are places I am missing because I have not traveled there yet. I am fully aware that I will miss someone or something that is vital to someone else who is in the tradition now.

I come to this page and the ones that follow with an open heart and a willingness to offer what I know - so far. May it be a spell of possibility and an entry point for your exploring heart. May you find what you seek. May you delight in the spaces that remain mysterious.

A Welcome

When you come to a ritual or a class, we often begin with a welcome, a way to bring people together to understand what they are about to experience and what they need to know about the culture of Reclaiming.

Welcome. Welcome to this space and time. Welcome to a journey of Reclaiming Witchcraft.

I first begin by honoring those who held the land I walk upon and rest upon, those who cultivated the land and honored it. I acknowledge that the land upon which I write is of the Wappo, Southern Pomo, and Graton Rancheria. These indigenous peoples are those who stewarded the land before and whose culture remains alive today.

May the work of my magick in Reclaiming be an act of reciprocity and healing. May our continued acknowledgement of the land and its people of before, now, and tomorrow offer a blessing.

As you read through this book, you will notice that it focuses on the history, the beliefs, the structures, the courses, and some of the key ideas of Reclaiming. While we are a living tradition that is often passed down orally in classes, this book strives to give some insights into the way Reclaiming groups and Witches often (not always!) practice.

But this is not a book of magickal practice. And as you will learn, saying there is one practice for every Reclaiming Witch is unrealistic.

Things to know about Reclaiming right now

Our public rituals and classes are clean and sober. We seek to change our consciousness at will, so we need the fullness of our will at all times. This does not mean that all Reclaiming Witches are in recovery or are clean and sober. We strive to support our beloveds in recovery by making our rituals and classes free from intoxicants.

We maintain confidentiality. We do not share stories or pictures of others unless we have their express permission to do so. Not everyone is out of the broom closet, nor do they want their information shared in public.

We are an ecstatic and participatory tradition. We seek to have embodied magickal experiences that are not focused on a high priestess/priest model. While there might be ritual leaders, everyone is encouraged to participate at the level that feels good to them.

We strive to make all events accessible. Our classes and rituals are sliding scale, meaning they are offered at a range of rates, based on ability to pay, without the need to provide proof of income. Many classes and camps offer scholarships or work trade opportunities. If there are any issues with physical access, we are eager to learn how we can help support as many people as possible, knowing there are budget/site limitations in some cases.

We seek to remember that we are all doing our best. We can meet each other where we are, without trying to change or fix each other. But we still hold each other accountable for our actions - and their impact, no matter the intention.

Welcome.

Magickal Beginning

Charge of the Goddess
Traditional by Doreen Valiente, as adapted by Starhawk:

Listen to the words of the Great Mother, Who of old was called Artemis, Astarte, Dione, Melusine, Aphrodite, Cerridwen, Diana, Arionrhod, Brigid, and by many other names:

Whenever you have need of anything, once a month, and better it be when the moon is full, you shall assemble in some secret place and adore the spirit of Me Who is Queen of all the Wise.

You shall be free from slavery, and as a sign that you be free you shall be naked in your rites.

Sing, feast, dance, make music and love, all in My Presence, for Mine is the ecstasy of the spirit and Mine also is joy on earth.

For My law is love is unto all beings. Mine is the secret that opens the door of youth, and Mine is the cup of wine of life that is the cauldron of Cerridwen, that is the holy grail of immortality.

I give the knowledge of the spirit eternal, and beyond death I give peace and freedom and reunion with those that have gone before.

Nor do I demand aught of sacrifice, for behold, I am the Mother of all things and My love is poured out upon the earth.

Hear the words of the Star Goddess, the dust of Whose feet are the hosts of Heaven, whose body encircles the universe:

I Who am the beauty of the green earth and the white moon among the stars and the mysteries of the waters,

I call upon your soul to arise and come unto me.

For I am the soul of nature that gives life to the universe.

From Me all things proceed and unto Me they must return.

Let My worship be in the heart that rejoices, for behold, all acts of love and pleasure are My rituals.

Let there be beauty and strength, power and compassion, honor and humility, mirth and reverence within you.

And you who seek to know Me, know that the seeking and yearning will avail you not, unless you know the Mystery: for if that which you seek, you find not within yourself, you will never find it without.

For behold, I have been with you from the beginning, and I am That which is attained at the end of desire.

I start with this as it is has become a part of my foundation as a Witch and as a Reclaiming Witch. I have said it enough times that my bones know the delight of each word. And the charge that it is has become the charge I take forward.

Chapter 1

The Beginning / History

The story of Reclaiming and its history have many threads and many forces that have driven it to the place it is today. To attempt to explain it would be to miss something, to not tell all of the stories from different perspectives. Yet, remembering where we came from is an important place to begin.

At most rituals, those leading the ritual will ask if there is anyone who has not been to a Reclaiming ritual before. When there are many hands that go up, the story is told something like this:

Reclaiming began in the 1980s with Starhawk and Diane Baker teaching classes in San Francisco, California, USA to people who wanted to do their own rituals. These classes started as the *Elements of Magick* class, informed by Starhawk's 'The Spiral Dance: a Rebirth of the Ancient Religion of the Great Goddess' (later referenced as 'Spiral Dance' in this book) and the themes of 'Dreaming the Dark'. In these classes, people began to experience the wonder of collective magick, the way to practice magick, and how to build rituals in groups or individually.

From there, the students were coming and completing the class, and then wanting more. Since Starhawk had studied with Victor and Cora Anderson of the Feri Tradition, the tools of *Iron Pentacle* and *Pearl Pentacle* became new classes to offer. And eventually, *Rites of Passage* became another class.

During this period, Reclaiming continued to grow and expand, but became so big that it started to be necessary to dissolve the Collective as it was in that time. It was too large and too focused in one area, and to expand the power amongst all those who were interested in this tradition, the *Principles of Unity* were created as a way to have some sort of definition of

Reclaiming.

The *Principles of Unity* was birthed in 1997, and Reclaiming spread as communities further afield than the San Francisco area. More classes were birthed, new camps were begun, and ongoing conversations about diversity and activism continued. Today, the communities are across the United States, Canada, Brazil, Europe, and Australia.

The Threads that Brought Us Here

A way to bring Reclaiming into context is to look at the different movements that rose or came into focus at the same time. All of these practices informed the construction of many practices that still exist today and the emergence of a witchcraft tradition.

Return to the Goddess

During the time of the initial beginnings of Reclaiming, the re-emergence of Goddess spirituality opened the door. People began to turn to the idea of the Mother Earth and away from the monotheistic way that Christianity looked at the world.

Instead of the traditional images of subservient woman and male god, perhaps spirituality could look different, more maternal, softer and less aggressive. Of course, this is not to say that all looked at goddess spirituality in the same way. After all, Athena and Freya are warriors too.

Some sources will cite the emergence of goddess spirituality as being in the 1970s, with movements across multiple countries and continents, not just North America. Others will point to certain people, including Carol P. Christ and Z Budapest as being influencers of their time.

One might also want to keep in mind that the idea of Goddess was subversive and called into focus the idea of a deity who could birth and renew and nourish, the opposite of the male god figure, the paternal, distant taskmaster.

Feminism

We can also turn to the various waves of feminism as being a wind in the sails of the movement toward Reclaiming. With the Goddess-based spirituality movement and the first wave of feminism transitioning into the second wave in the 1960s, there was greater focus upon inequality and workplace issues, as well as reproductive rights, distribution of power in families, and legal problems. In those times of unrest and more outspoken voices, it became clear that bonding together would help advance the causes of that time. (And while we have moved into the third and fourth waves of feminism now, we see the place from which the tradition was shaped in the cauldron of society's movements.)

Feri Witchcraft

As mentioned before, the Feri tradition of Witchcraft also influenced the movement of Reclaiming. Within 'Spiral Dance' are descriptions of Feri tools, like *Iron Pentacle* and *Pearl Pentacle*, as well as the concept of the three souls. These tools were inspirations for other core classes in Reclaiming and aided in the ongoing self-development of community members.

Feri, with its emphasis on personal work and explorations of power, became an important part of the magick of Reclaiming. While not all Reclaiming Witches would call themselves Feri witches, the influence of there being places of shadow and shine, as well as different connections within the same experience show up in ritual and classes today. (It is also worthwhile to note that some feel that Reclaiming is a branch of Feri Witchcraft, but this is not something that is true for all - or true for those outside of Reclaiming.)

Activism & Politics

While 'Spiral Dance' was written and published in 1979, one must remember this was the time of Reagan's imminent inauguration into office. People were scared of what might happen next, how that choice of president might harm the world and the future.

Groups began to gather in their despair and their grief. They gave their anger to cauldrons and to water; they gave these energies so that they might be transformed into something useful in the times no one could predict. They came together in ritual. They came together so they would never feel alone.

More groups formed in solidarity. Covens (Compost, Wind Hags, Coven Raving) formed and fell then sprung up again in other forms. For example, there was a ritual of grief and solidarity that happened at Antioch College in 1981 after the election of Reagan, which eventually became the Brigid Ritual as it is celebrated today.

Community members came together to protest at Diablo Canyon in 1981. At this point, classes in Reclaiming had already started and new classes were starting to take shape. The action at Diablo Canyon was in direct response to the development of nuclear power, and it was also a place where the members of 'almost' Reclaiming were learning about to organize protests and actions, how to use consensus, and how to work magick together as a group.

From those organizing efforts at Diablo, the group came back and solidified the idea of the Reclaiming Collective - or the structure by which the initial tradition began to take shape. Later on, Reclaiming, now a tradition, would protest in Livermore and create a blockade to prevent the morning meetings at the 1999 WTO.

Reclaiming was brought together by the times, by the folks who stood up and stood with each other. Through the combination of coven work and political actions and organizing, Reclaiming was the tradition that didn't start off to be one, as many founding members have shared. They simply came together to do what was right for the world and for each other.

Chapter 2

Principles of Unity / Beliefs

"My law is love unto all beings..."
– from *'The Charge of the Goddess'* by Doreen Valiente

The values of the Reclaiming tradition stem from our understanding that **the earth is alive and all of life is sacred and interconnected**. We see the Goddess as immanent in the earth's cycles of birth, growth, death, decay and regeneration. Our practice arises from a deep, spiritual commitment to the earth, to healing and to the linking of magic with political action.

Each of us embodies the divine. Our ultimate spiritual authority is within, and we need no other person to interpret the sacred to us. **We foster the questioning attitude, and honor intellectual, spiritual and creative freedom.**

We are an evolving, dynamic tradition and proudly call ourselves Witches. Our diverse practices and experiences of the divine weave a tapestry of many different threads. We include those who honor Mysterious Ones, Goddesses, and Gods of myriad expressions, genders, and states of being, remembering that mystery goes beyond form. Our community rituals are participatory and ecstatic, celebrating the cycles of the seasons and our lives, and raising energy for personal, collective and earth healing.

We know that everyone can do the life-changing, world-renewing work of magic, the art of changing consciousness at will. We strive to teach and practice in ways that foster personal and collective empowerment, to model shared power and to open leadership roles to all. We make decisions by consensus, and balance individual autonomy with social responsibility.

Our tradition honors the wild, and calls for service to the earth and the community. We value peace and practice non-violence, in keeping with the Rede, "Harm none, and do what you will." We work for all forms of justice: environmental, social, political, racial, gender and economic. Our feminism includes a radical analysis of power, seeing all systems of oppression as interrelated, rooted in structures of domination and control.

We welcome all genders, all gender histories, all races, all ages and sexual orientations and all those differences of life situation, background, and ability that increase our diversity. **We strive to make our public rituals and events accessible and safe. We try to balance the need to be justly compensated for our labor with our commitment to make our work available to people of all economic levels.**

All living beings are worthy of respect. All are supported by the sacred elements of air, fire, water and earth. We work to **create and sustain communities and cultures that embody our values, that can help to heal the wounds of the earth and her peoples, and that can sustain us and nurture future generations.**

Reclaiming Principles of Unity – consensed by the Reclaiming Collective in 1997. Updated at the BIRCH council meeting of Dandelion Gathering 5 in 2012.

When the Collective dissolved, it became important to more clearly define what a Reclaiming Witch was. After all, with a group growing so large, it was hard enough to get everyone into one space, even harder to get them to all agree on what they were.

And thus the *Principles of Unity* were discussed, created, argued, and consensed upon in a room that still exists today. A magickal room with a window that reveals the sky and the moon in certain times of the month. In times when the fog has not quite crept into view.

The *Principles of Unity* (a.k.a. POU) is the document that sought to bring forth the beliefs that encapsulated the tradition as it was at that moment in time. It also seeks to create a way forward for the magick we do as witches, to set the stage for what we hope to do in order to inspire and aid the future generations.

But something that was created in a smaller group over 20 years ago is not a document that held up to time and transitions in the community. The voices of Reclaiming members and their children began to speak up about the way they were not reflected in the original language. Those with different gender histories, those who did not identify with godds, those who were not clear if the POU was welcoming to them.

Conversations began to take place in the years before the Dandelion Gathering in Portland, Oregon, in 2012. Calls were made to communities across the world to discuss what the POU meant to them and what, if anything, was missing..

Voices shared their frustrations, their excitement, and their fears. Witches traveled from around the world to the gathering where a BIRCH meeting was held to help bring these views together in order to discuss potential changes to the POU. (After all, if there was no consensus to the changes, the POU would not change. And as BIRCH is the one meeting where these sorts of decisions are made, the discussion would have to rest until the next gathering…)

There were breakout groups and discussions and strong words and people who felt heard - and not heard. And in the magick of facilitation and many sheets of paper, the new POU was crafted and consensed on by those in attendance at that Dandelion.

The Importance of the POU

For those new to Reclaiming, there are a few things to remember about the POU - and there are many more ways to approach this document as you dive deeper into the magick.

1. The POU allows Reclaiming to answer this question: what makes a Reclaiming Witch a Reclaiming Witch? Because we are a non-initiatory tradition (thought we do have initiations), the only thing a person needs to do to call themselves a Reclaiming Witch is to agree to follow the POU. That's it.
2. The POU becomes the mission statement that you can use to come back to the core of Reclaiming's activism and motivations.

But what's also become important about the POU to more recent Reclaiming Witches is that it is the document that many of us looked to as a guide. And we watched it become a document that fell out of date with what our community began to look like.

In the moment where it was suggested that perhaps the document could change and would change with the will of the group, the POU became a place of coming together to adapt, to listen, and to hear. Because if nothing else is important about the POU to someone, the idea that it could change is something that enables the tradition to continue forward in supporting those who are called to the work.

It's also important to point out how the POU is not the perfect fit for everyone. Today, it is still debated for its new wording, for its current wording, and for the gaps that it doesn't address. In many classes where the POU is introduced or cited, teachers encourage conversations about what works - and what doesn't.

Perhaps in this ever-evolving tradition, we must expect to have a document that inspires some and challenges others. Perhaps it's healthy to have something that is criticized as much as it is revered.

Perhaps the beauty of an anarchist tradition is that when

you see something that doesn't work for you, you find ways to bring in what you need, to give voice to those who have not been heard, and to always ask the question: what else can we do?

The *Principles of Unity* might be likened to the way air pushes a boat along, giving direction, but those holding the ship's wheel are the ones who guide it to safety.

Chapter 3

Groups & Structures

While we've talked briefly about the history of Reclaiming and the overall beliefs that drive the community forward, how things work can be a little mysterious to the outside world. Often, Reclaiming is see as a group that doesn't have any structures because of its roots in anarchism and activism, as though it simply 'happens' instead of having groups in place to support various goals.

To be clear, when Reclaiming was a collective, things became a lot larger than expected and the original structure did dissolve. In its place, cells and groups grew. These formed in areas around the world, enabling Reclaiming to continue to grow and spread and be supported by those people in those areas.

As noted before, you need only agree to follow the *Principles of Unity* in order to call yourself a Reclaiming Witch. You can simply come to rituals, attend classes, hang out with other cool Witches, and be a part of community in that way.

There is no expectation when you start entering into the culture of Reclaiming. However, there are those who want to step into roles of organizing and planning. There are many who decide that stepping into teaching, planning, or organizing roles are the next best steps for them.

This is often called stepping into leadership and stepping into more responsibility for the tradition and its community.

Cells & Working Groups

One might join a group because they are interested in the particular work of a cell. There are cells for ritual planning within areas or for larger rituals (e.g. Spiral Dance). At the time of writing, there are also cells that support the non-profit requirements of Reclaiming (e.g. the Wheel), there are cells that include representatives of numerous cells to share ideas and to aid decision-making, there are cells that include teachers, etc. And there have been cells that spring up and then fall away until they are needed in the community again.

The Creation of a Cell

The group gets together, at first, to talk about the goals they have as a group. They might talk about what they want to do, how they want to do it, and how they might create a structure for their particular group. In the Reclaiming structure at the moment, there are ways to apply to become a 'full' cell that can have a representative on the Wheel (more on that in a moment).

Each proto-cell, as they're lovingly called before assuming full cell status, is asked to discuss and answer a series of 13 questions. These questions include everything from who the membership is, how people get into the cell, what the cell will do, how the cell will navigate conflict, and what the cell might need from the Wheel.

Once these questions are answered, the answers are given to the Wheel to discuss to see if the answers are complete. The representatives decide if the cell is accepted into the Wheel, and then pass on that decision.

Ritual Planning Cells

As they are the most common, let's look at Ritual Planning Cells (RPCs).

Ritual planning cells are present in a number of areas at this moment: Los Angeles, San Francisco, East Bay, North Bay, Portland, Baltimore, Seattle, Minneapolis, Pittsburgh, etc.

Though all cells, of course, are different in the way they approach their service or focus, ritual planning cells often work in this way.

Ritual planning cells are comprised of people who have taken classes, come to public rituals, and have become a part of the community in the area. These groups of people are often up to 13 in size, with rotation schedules to foster sustainability and shared power.

These cells will gather on a regular schedule to plan rituals for the Wheel of the Year, as they have agreed to support this calendar. Some groups will support all of the sabbats/ holidays, while others will support only some depending on community needs.

By using consensus decision-making process, the groups will share ideas, outline rituals, and then recruit people from community to take on roles. Since Reclaiming does not require anyone have certain training or be initiated to be a priestess, anyone is welcome and encouraged to lead as they are called.

The rituals happen at local venues and are often constructed to not only align with the holiday, but also with the specific needs of the community and the current events in the world. Ritual planning cells will not only plan rituals, but are often called on to help support other events in their areas, e.g. Dandelion, Spiral Dance Ritual, etc. These groups can be resources to other ritual planning cells.

The cells will also participate in ritual feedback gathering to aid each other in growing skill sets and effectiveness. These groups are also called on to help navigate community feedback and situations. In addition, the cells will also handle donations to support site and supply fees. These cells are working groups, though many members will have personal relationships and work together outside of the meeting space.

Unsurprisingly, different cells might have different rules about memberships, e.g. having taken *Elements of Magick* - or not. Some cells are comprised of teachers, so the members need to be present or past community teachers who apply to be a part of the group.

To become a member of a cell in Reclaiming, you will inquire with the group about what they ask of you and what they want you to come into the cell knowing. Not only does this help the cell as a whole, it also helps to ease the transition into the space.

In many cases, there are people who will help mentor new members to ensure they understand the meeting schedule, the roles of everyone, etc.

Some groups might have an ally membership, which is a starting point. In North Bay Reclaiming, for example, you can join the ritual planning cell as an ally. This allows you to be in that role for a year and be fully involved in the decision-making and planning processes. You have the time to decide if the group is a good fit for everyone before committing to a longer term as a full member. Usually, newer members are just asked not to block any decisions or to be involved in certain decisions until they are a full member.

Wheel

At the center of all of the groups in Reclaiming is the Wheel. Since Reclaiming is a non-profit organization, it needs to have a Board of Directors. And since we're a non-hierarchical tradition, that's tricky. So, the Wheel is in place to help guide the larger questions about money, legalities, etc. in Reclaiming. Cells send representatives to these Wheels where they can discuss their group needs and requests, as well as help in decision-making for the greater Reclaiming area.

As of writing this book, the Wheel is located in the San Francisco Bay Area, with representatives from cells in California. Members rotate out to make room for new members and decisions are always made by consensus process.

The minutes of meetings are compiled for anyone to review, as this is part of the non-profit status. They often include agenda items about how to manage the budget and bank accounts of Reclaiming, how to navigate tricky situations and requests (e.g.

people might request the backing of Reclaiming for an event or they might reach out for permission to use a certain text), and what each community is facing - and how they might need support.

At quarterly meetings, the Wheel comes together to find out how they can best support greater Reclaiming in that moment. Since Reclaiming started in the San Francisco Bay Area, this is where the Wheel has been present, and there are discussions in place about how to expand the representation and how to potentially focus on a wider area than the Bay Area.

How can you support the needs of all communities? How can you have balanced representation across time zones and miles/kilometers? That is a question Reclaiming continues to ponder.

Event Organizers

There might also be cells that work to organize larger events in the Reclaiming community. The most frequent events are:

- Spiral Dance Ritual
- Camps
- Dandelion Gatherings

Spiral Dance

The Spiral Dance Ritual originated at the same time the book, 'The Spiral Dance', came out in 1979. This ritual was originally held in the Women's Building in San Francisco at Samhain. Thousands of people would gather to travel to the Isle of Apples to meet with their Beloved Dead and to celebrate the Witches' New Year.

Needless to say, organizing and planning the Spiral Dance ritual is a complex, multi-step process that takes place over six to eight months. There is a Spiral Dance cell that works hard to make sure the ritual site is secured, the contracts are in place, the schedule is firm, and the ritual is planned and 'staffed' by priestesses.

The Spiral Dance cell (and other cells) will also use smaller working groups called charettes. These smaller groups are empowered by the larger group to make decisions, while bringing them back to the group when they are ready to share their outcomes. This process frees the entire group from having to make every decisions and encourages trust among all groups to move forward with plans that need to be completed on a timeline.

Those on the Spiral Dance cell (and all cells) are volunteers who work to plan, but also to be on site during the ritual itself, ensuring that setup happens seamlessly, that ritualists are fed, that the ritual is practiced ahead of time, that lights and sound are working, etc. It's an all day, all night process that requires commitment and a dedication to service.

Camps

Reclaiming currently has Witchcamps that take place on three continents over the course of a year. These camps each have teams that help to organize the logistics, the advertising, the onsite activities, the magick, and the cleanup.

The word that's often used for camp leaders and coordinators is organizer, or someone who helps play an instrumental role in making sure camp happens. This is a role that is a sometimes a volunteer and sometimes a paid position, which often requires year-round engagement. In some camps, there are also weavers and spinners, those who take on different parts of organizing roles, some that deal more with magick and some that deal more with the mundane.

In all of these roles, camp organizers interface with each other, with teachers, and with campers. The organizers will communicate with each other to talk about selecting and/or writing the story for the camp, asking for teacher applications, hiring teachers, managing money, managing the things they didn't expect to come up, etc. Some organizers will focus primarily on before-camp details, while others might be on the ground during camp to attend to needs as they arise. These organizers will work with the teachers and often a 'lead/continuity' teacher to make sure the teachers have what they need, e.g. the story, the budget, the schedule, logistics, travel arrangements, etc.

If it sounds like a difficult job, it often is. Some camps will have 100+ campers, which leads to many needs and requests to manage. At the same time, organizers are instrumental in holding the magickal container of camp. They often do magick before camp begins, calling the right story to the work, energetically reaching out to possible teachers and campers, doing abundance magick, leading fundraising efforts, etc.

The teachers are the other group that help play a major role in Witchcamps. They are usually hired through an application process. Organizers review applications to decide if the applicants are the best fit.

The teachers and organizers will interface with each other to bring the camp into reality over the course of six to eight months. They will work out any issues, troubleshoot situations, and be ready to hold the camp as it unfolds over four to seven days.

Dandelion Gatherings

Every few years, Dandelion Gatherings occur to help bring disparate communities together. These gatherings are held in more central locations and often organized by members of multiple communities to talk about larger issues in Reclaiming. It is a time for connecting with people you may never see in person or to discuss issues with far-reaching impact. More recent Dandelion Gatherings have been held in Portland, Oregon, USA in 2012 and Petaluma, California, USA in 2019.

These gatherings are designed to be as sustainable and affordable as possible to encourage more participation. For those who are in far-off communities, there are scholarships and often fundraisers to help get more voices in the room.

These Dandelion Gatherings have led to important decisions and shifts in Reclaiming as a whole. At the gathering in 2012, the *Principles of Unity* was updated and changed to bring in more inclusive language. This required various working groups to discuss different points of the document and to bring forward ideas until they could be agreed upon with everyone who was in the room by consensus process.

Also at these gatherings are BIRCH meetings. BIRCH (Broad-Intra-Reclaiming Council of Hubs) is a group of representatives from groups around the world that can only make decisions in person at these meetings when they're held. The require people to show up to represent their groups and if decisions cannot be made, they will need to wait until the next meeting.

Presently, the limited meeting time has brought up new conversations about whether this is a model that works well at the present moment. Some have pointed out that as Dandelion Gatherings have only happened in North America, the representative has been uneven in terms of the entire Reclaiming community around the world. Perhaps in the future, BIRCH may look completely different.

Even More

Within Reclaiming are groups like the Witchcamp Council which acts like the Wheel for Witchcamps. It is the central hub that includes representatives of camps and guilds (e.g. teaching groups) within the tradition. Like other groups, the council meets regularly online, but then has in-person meetings to help foster more connections.

There are groups that do not seek to be consensed into the Wheel's structure. And there are cells that go quiet. There are cells who focus on the needs of their communities. There are cells that come together monthly, yearly, in-person and online.

And to be clear, a lot of these structures and groups involve meetings. Lots of meetings. These are the things that happen behind the rituals and the camps and the classes that people see first when they're entering the Reclaiming community.

While this might not seem to be the most exciting part of magick, without a container to hold and support the energy, the enthusiasm, and the commitment of Reclaiming folks, there might be a lot of conversation - and not as much action.

Chapter 4

Your Own Spiritual Authority / How to Practice

When you're first in a class in Reclaiming, or sometimes this is mentioned at public rituals, you will hear the phrase:

You are your own spiritual authority in community.

It is often explained as the notion that if you need to move your body or act in a certain way to make the magick work for you, do it (so long as you're not negatively impacting someone else's experience). If you like to trance standing up, do it. If you need to leave a ritual because you're not feeling it anymore, do it.

If you need to do _____ , go for it but be mindful of others as you do.

To some this is an invitation for expression, while others feel this statement is a large permission slip for confusion.

The Typical Reclaiming Witch

This could be the shortest explanation of a Witch you'll ever see: there is no typical Reclaiming Witch. More often than not, a Reclaiming Witch will follow the POU, may attend public rituals, and likely has taken *Elements of Magick* at some point.

But if you look around the community that you may be close to or that you might visit, you will notice a wide range of Witches. From young to old, from polytheistic to nontheistic, from trans to cis, introvert to extrovert, activist to parent, and on and on - we are a diverse bunch.

The good news is that the lack of a 'right way' to do Reclaiming is liberating, but for those who are new to Witchcraft in general, it can also be confusing.

And this is where I feel the part of Reclaiming that is about self-empowerment comes into action. Where we find ourselves in relationship to the Elements, we find ourselves in our relationship with the Earth. We bring into focus the way we relate to ourselves and our shadows in *Iron Pentacle*, and with community in *Pearl Pentacle*.

As we move into more experience of community, the Communities Class offers a place for holding each other in this process, just as Rites enables us to celebrate our movement from one point of time to the present or the future.

Though you can certainly empower yourself without a class, it seems to me that Reclaiming offers places to sink deeply inward and to reach out a hand to someone else. In doing so, the pull between the inner and the outer enables the discovery of the center, of the place where YOU are.

You find yourself in relationship to yourself, to the being you are becoming and the being you already are.

Practice as You Will

I certainly can't speak to the experience of all Reclaiming Witches, but I can share with you the practices I feel have been inspired by or motivated by Reclaiming Witchcraft.

Daily Practice

I was taught early on in my Reclaiming life that having a daily practice was the thing to prioritize. This might look like 10 minutes every day where you do something that is devotional, physical, spiritual, etc. It might look like an hour or it might look like 15 minutes a few times a day. What is important is the routine, the commitment, and the showing-up-when-you-really-don't-feel-like-it.

Daily practice is the opportunity to connect into your own spiritual authority and what brings you back to you. In the midst of chaos or, well, life, you can return to your daily practice as something consistent and steady.

I have varied my daily practice over the years. It's included incense and prayers to various deities. I've also used practices from other traditions I study as part of my daily practice. I've also used cleaning and song as a daily practice. Or divination with runes or tarot. Or daily pages, a la Julia Cameron. Or walking. Or meditate. Or listen to a song. Or drum...

Find a daily practice that works for you and make it simple enough that you can't come up with an excuse to skip it. Then do it again and again until you feel you want to do more or do something else. Do it until it becomes what you do versus the thing you must do.

Allow daily practice to be equally invigorating and boring. Let it be the thing you resist and fall into. See what happens when you keep showing up.

Altars

Right now, I can't think of a Reclaiming Witch I know who doesn't have some sort of altar in their living space. It might not be large or filled with expensive statues, but there's an altar somewhere (probably in many witches' homes). We talk about creating altars, we create altars during classes, we create altars for rituals, etc.

Like daily practice, altars can become the place of focus and commitment. You create space for something in your life, e.g. a deity or many deities, a particular working you're doing, a seasonal altar, etc. It could be a place of offerings to a deity you want to build a relationship with. It could be a place to put pretty things as an altar of gratitude. Or you might put out things you associate with the various sabbats. Or something else.

It doesn't have to be filled with expensive things. It doesn't have to be complicated. There are no rules to making your altar. But I can say that once you make one, you're likely to make another. And another. And another.

27

Rituals

To bring myself back to the magick, to bring myself back when it's not connecting with me or I'm feeling as though my life is out of sorts, I return to ritual. I return to the turns of the wheel and the moments of ecstasy. I come to the places where those who identify with Reclaiming (no matter what that looks like) come together to celebrate, to heal, to mourn, and to dance together. I come back to the places where I can remember I am not alone. Sometimes, I need to be in the presence of others to fully know myself as connected to the web of life.

I may not go to every ritual, or I might. I might celebrate on my own with small groups or I might celebrate in other ways, outside of the wheel of the year. I've been a part of rites of passage (first blood, blessingway, croning, initiations, grief rituals, celebration rituals, etc.) and I've been part of smaller moments of ritual - spontaneous and vital.

Being in magick space with others is nourishing and restoring. While I can certainly perform ritual on my own, when I am in contact with others, I remember being a part of something bigger. I can hold space for myself and for others. I can extend the strength of magick and create spells of resilience. I can touch back to these ritual moments where I was freed from my loneliness - or maybe just reminded I never needed to be lonely in the first place. (And not everyone feels this way. Not everyone talks about the rituals they do that act as opportunities to resource themselves during hard moments of their lives.)

Some nights, I just look up at the moon and whisper my fears and my joys. Sometimes I visit the ocean and know the waves will hear what my heart says in each beat.

Relationship Building

Another common part of Reclaiming Witchcraft is the building of relationships. This might be with humans, with the Earth, or with the Divine. It might also include relationships with the

Beloved Dead, the Mighty Dead, or the Ancestors. Or something else. Someone else. For a long period of time or for a short period of time.

Let's list some potential candidates for relationships:

- Fellow humans and witches
- The Elements of Air, Fire, Water, Earth, and Center/Spirit
- The Fae
- Spirits of the Land
- Time
- States of Being - Grief, Joy, Passion, Grace, Creativity, Power, etc.
- Purpose - anti-racism, trans rights and activism, safety for POC and trans bodies, earth activism, etc.
- Ancestors - Blood, Bone, Spirit, Heart, Activism, etc.
- Beloved Dead - those of our blood who have died, those who are our family and who we call as part of our lineage
- Mighty Dead - the ancestors of Craft, those who have inspired our Witchcraft and Magick, those who have been in our training and initiation lineage, those who have shaped us into Witches
- Deities / Gods / Goddesses / Godds / Mysterious Ones

And you might have other ideas about relationships that you seek to cultivate.

From calling out to them or answering their call, you can begin to come into contact. You might start altars for your relationship or for offerings to these relations. You might set aside time to open yourself to feeling their wisdom sink into your consciousness. You might go out on walks or adventures with them to learn more.

You come to the relationship with your needs, your boundaries, and your questions. You show up to see how this progresses. You might start a relationships that is strong at the start and then fades away. Or you might start a lifelong relationship that shifts over the years.

The practice of being in relationship informs Reclaiming magick by reminding us that any relationship requires our attention and our dedication. We can't simply say we're in a relationship or an ally to someone/something without doing some work.

Community Gatherings & Common Purposes

One of the things I learned pretty quickly in Reclaiming is that the more you show up, the more you will be asked to do. While I have also learned to temper this with the reality of self-care and boundaries, what is important about this advice is that showing up is how one can be a part of community.

You may not always show up as your best self, and you may not always show up as your happiest self, but showing up in all of your pieces and parts is part of the magick. Our magick, anyone's magick, will never be perfect, and when we show up in this imperfection and curiosity, we can allow ourselves to be a part of what happens now and next.

And there are many community gatherings that have happened over the years. Planned by community members or community groups, these gatherings have fostered conversations and plans for new groups. And, sometimes, gatherings just look like potluck where you eat, you laugh, and you enjoy each other.

There are stories of many potlucks that turned into cells and that led to larger conversations in the tradition. And these happened because people showed up, said what was true, heard what was hard, and tried to find a way to hold each other well. And certainly failed at times. But still showed up.

Impact vs. Intention

Since many of the people reading this book may not have hands-on experience of Reclaiming (yet!?), it is important to note that

Reclaiming has often shared the idea of thinking well of each other. We have often said in classes and camps that we should always assume the best intention of each other before we move into a space of disagreement or anger.

But this conversation has shifted in recent years. One might say that we think well of each other AND hold each other accountable in the presence of someone being hurt in the process.

Most of us don't intend to hurt anyone with our words or our actions. We want the best for ourselves and we want the best for others. Our minds, in their best moments, want nothing more than to support those we love - and even those we have a harder time loving.

But we fail. We have great intentions, and emotions get in the way. And our defensiveness gets in the way. And our reaction to the possibility of hurting someone else gets in the way. We fall back to our intention, saying, 'Of course I didn't mean it like that....' It's not a lie, but if the impact was something else, we will need to take responsibility for the harm we have caused.

I bring this up also because the idea of being one's own spiritual authority can sound as though anything goes. And that's not untrue. But when you add 'in community' at the end, your actions and their impact become a part of the process.

In the use of consensus (more on this later) to facilitate conversations and decision-making in Reclaiming, we can often ensure the best possible interactions between folx. And we will have conflict. It cannot be stressed enough how our humanity can be upsetting in a community of well-meaning humans.

One way that we can navigate conflicts in community is to follow a process that has been in place for the North Bay Reclaiming Ritual Planning Cell in California, USA.

1. Discuss the conflict within 24 - 72 hours with the person you are in conflict with.
2. If the conflict cannot be resolved, bring the conflict to the

31

cell.

3. If the conflict cannot be resolved within the cell, bring in a third-party meditator.

4. If the conflict cannot be resolved, the cell might ask the person to leave or hold a consensus decision that involved a vote not including the person who started the conflict. Or two people involved in the conflict.

Many cells and groups will come up with a conflict resolution process that they can use to start movement toward resolution and, hopefully, healing. There are also structures for constructive feedback to help communicate opportunities for growth. Because of the desire to continue to look at impact vs. intention, open communication is vital for progress. And these are structures that may not work in all cases and there might be opportunities to bring difficult conversations into ritual space to see what magick can teach us about resolution.

As a Reclaiming Witch, and really as a human, we strive to be inclusive of the spiritual authority and expertise of each other in community. You may not agree with everything everyone does - and we certainly are unique in our approaches, even after studying under the same teachers from the same books.

Yes, this is what makes us Reclaiming Witches hard to define from the outside, to be sure. And this is why it's so important to experience a tradition of witchcraft from the inside at a ritual or a class before starting to define what it is.

Chapter 5

Ritual

Reclaiming offers public rituals around the world at all times of the year. While many will follow the traditional Wheel of the Year as seen in pagan books and other communities, there are some communities that might work a little differently. For example, one community plans a Spring, Summer, Fall, and Winter ritual each year, while another might plan up to eight rituals a year in alignment with the Wheel of the Year.

To make sense of what Reclaiming does, here is a wider view of ritual, its schedule, its essence, and its structure. And as with everything, when you attend a ritual, you might see something completely different, depending on the input of those who planned it and those who showed up to bring their own magick.

Wheel of the Year

In Reclaiming, we typically follow the cycle of the year as inspired by the Celtic seasons and the movement of the sun. That said, depending on where you are located in Reclaiming, these rituals can happen at different times of the year or they can be informed by the local weather and growing patterns.

Remember, there are Reclaiming groups in the northern and southern hemispheres, which leads to 'opposite' observances when one witch celebrates Samhain as the other celebrates Beltane - the mirror of celebrating death and life.

Samhain

The wheel begins with Samhain on October 31 in the Northern Hemisphere and April 30/May 1 in the Southern Hemisphere. This time of meeting with the Beloved Dead, those who have passed on in previous years, is both celebratory and solemn. A time of remembering and grieving, but also a time of connecting and visiting the realms as the veil between the worlds is thin.

Winter Solstice / Yule

On December 20/21/22 (Northern Hemisphere) and June 20/21/22 (Southern Hemisphere), we celebrate the time of the longest night, the time when the light begins to shift, bringing the song of hope for returning light.

Brigid / Imbolc

Around February 1 or 2 (Northern Hemisphere) and August 1 (Southern Hemisphere), the celebration of Brigid or Imbolc begins. This is the time when the spring is started to reveal itself, a time when the light be growing and plants begin to rise up from the ground. Often in Reclaiming, we will celebrate Brigid instead of Imbolc as this is a ritual that began at the time in the US when Reagan was elected.

In all of the despair and grief of the election, some witches gathered in the San Francisco Bay area to dream into how to use their magick to move through the despair and into action. They stayed up all night on the Winter Solstice and decided to do a ritual for action on the next pagan holiday: Brigid. They created a ritual that brought forward fears and transformed them, and then brought forward the places of action and made commitments over water and fire (candles) to move forward. Over time, this has become a ritual for Brigid, to make a pledge to her and to community at the well and at the forge/flame.

Ostara / Spring Equinox

On March 21/22 (Northern Hemisphere) or September 21/22 (Southern Hemisphere), the light finds balance. It is at the point of potential and tipping into light. This is the place of promise and springtime and newness. Often, this is a ritual where children can go on egg hunts and sometimes the names of babies who have been born are read into the ritual.

Beltane / May Day

On May 1 (Northern Hemisphere) and October 31/November 1 (Southern Hemisphere), it's time for Beltane. In most rituals, the group will celebrate life and fertility and creation by dancing around a Maypole. While in some traditions, this is a ritual that is focused on the heteronormative ideas of sexuality, Reclaiming strives to expand this idea and to engage inclusivity. Perhaps we don't work with fertility and we might work with creativity or passion. Or perhaps we have rituals that celebrate sexuality in all of its expressions and offer healing to those who are unable to fully express their love.

Litha / Summer Solstice

During June 20/21/22 (Northern Hemisphere) and December 20/21/22, we turn the wheel again to the longest day. On this day, we feel the extension of light strength across, with the knowledge that the darkness will creep in more and more each day. This is a time of celebration and wonder, a time of staying up as long as possible to soak in the height of warmth.

Lughnasadh / Lammas

On August 1 (Northern Hemisphere) and February 1 or 2 (Southern Hemisphere), Reclaiming will celebrate the first harvest, the time when things are beginning to calm and cool as the light diminishes. This can be a ritual of feasting and games, often taking some inspiration from Lugh or focusing on the cycle of farming.

Mabon / Fall Equinox

Around September 20/21 (Northern Hemisphere) and March 21/22 (Southern Hemisphere), the wheel turns once more to the place of ever-growing darkness and balance. It is clear that the year is changing and the second harvest is ready to be gathered. This is the time when we might realize all that we did has come to fruition - or we may realize we did not prepare enough for the coming darkness.

While these dates shift and are celebrated based on calendars, site availability, and group preference, these rituals help to bring communities together. It is hoped that rituals are the place of gathering, but not the only places of community. Perhaps they can serve as inspiration for activism, for action, and for groups to form into their own magickal support systems.

EIEIO

One of the things you will learn in Reclaiming as you begin to encounter rituals is the structure of what Reclaiming rituals do versus other traditions. We are an ecstatic tradition, one that wants to commune with the divine and our own divinity through embodiment and experience. Though not everyone needs to dance and sing or drum to feel ecstatic, there are some principles we use to create opportunities for ecstasy.

The idea of EIEIO emerged as a framework to keep in mind as we create rituals:

Ecstatic: We seek to plan rituals that connect bodies with ecstasy, knowing there are many versions of this and many ways to access the divine. In ritual, we might engage in various ritual technologies that support expansion of awareness and consciousness, as well as engagement with each other and the godds.

Improvisational: Because we are an ever-evolving tradition, we value the idea of improvisation. This is not to say that rituals are not planned, but rather we seek to be open to the possibility that something might arise as a need within a ritual. We encourage ritualists and participants to follow their spiritual authority to say or do what needs to be said or done.

Ensemble: In staying away from the high priest/priestess structure, we create rituals in groups, with multiple people taking on roles and rotating in those roles. For example, a person might help lead a trance in one ritual, but someone else might do it the next time. Ritual planning groups welcome people of all levels to support rituals and to volunteer to help.

Inspired: We offer rituals that are inspirational, often inspired by our own stories, ancient myths, interpretations of those myths, reactions to world events, etc. Rituals are often shifted based on what is happening in the present moment vs. needing to stick to a script.

Organic: Like inspiration, we create these rituals sometimes collaboratively and in the moment and sometimes in groups where we listen to the godds for guidance. Things emerge not from attachment or agenda, but from being open enough to hear what needs to be a part of ritual. We might also be open to what a community needs or shift a ritual based on something that has happened which might need tending or support.

While this list/acronym includes five areas, there are certainly others that Reclaiming ritualists and ritual planners try to keep in mind.

I would add: collaboration, vulnerability, safety, and inclusion. Rituals strive to be collaborative efforts among those who come and those who plan. When someone steps into the circle, they are just as important as anyone who steps into planning meetings. Folks who come can offer suggestions and drop into run-throughs to help support their/our community.

Vulnerability is a part of ritual that is offered as part of safety. I think Reclaiming rituals offer spaces of opening and revealing because we also offer safety. This is not to say that every ritual is perfectly safe, but we strive to make things safer. There have been times when things have happened in rituals that caused distress for participants. Those situations were navigated in the best ways possible - although sometimes they were not and became learning experiences.

Safety begins with the space and roles that are there to help people feel secure. There are often graces who act to welcome and cleanse those who come to rituals, often aiding with other transitions in rituals as well. There are also dragons, for example, that can help to answer questions and engage with people who are disruptive, not sober, or causing harm in some other way.

In fact, all ritual participants are empowered to support each other. While there might be one voice or one group that leads a part of the sacred space, everyone in the room can offer their energy to build the sacred container. And together, that container can hold everyone.

What a Reclaiming Ritual (Could) Look Like

Let's dispense with the 'not every Reclaiming ritual looks like this' disclaimer first. Many rituals do follow a certain structure as this is what creates consistency without asking for liturgy.

These pieces may all show up, often in this order, sometimes not.

Cleansing

Ritual begins with an opportunity to cleanse away the detritus of the world, both physically and psychically. Sometimes, this can look like using a smoke of a native plant or water or even a drum to clear things away. Most often, this cleansing process is held by graces who will also welcome people into the space with this moment of blessing.

Indigenous Acknowledgement

Depending on where you are located in the world, this piece

might also be called Welcome to Country. Before we do anything in ritual, we acknowledge the land upon which we stand and the land which was held by native peoples. We call out their names, we offer our gratitude and blessing, and we remember that many were lost and many still remain. This is a practice that is continuing to evolve in Reclaiming, and it offers a space of remembering colonization and its impact on the Earth.

Welcome

In public rituals, we offer a space of welcoming to those who have arrived and made the journey to participate. We give logistical information, ritual information, etiquette, and teach songs that will be used in the magick. This might also be a place where we welcome those new to Reclaiming and point out graces and dragons who can offer support. We also share the intention of the ritual with the promise that if a person needs to leave at any time as they can't support this intention, they are free to do so - no questions asked.

Grounding

And then we ground. We move into the space of becoming fully present in our bodies. We let go of what came before, what is about to happen, and what will happen later. We drop down into the earth for nourishment and we reach up to the skies for inspiration, and we bring those energies together as a reminder of the place we stand between. We remind ourselves that should we need energy for ritual, we do not need to deplete ourselves. Instead, we can draw upon the energies around us.

Casting

To create the container and to define the container for magick, we cast a circle. In the Reclaiming tradition (mostly), we start in the North. This is the space of earth and reverence, and we move to the East, to the South, to the West, and back to the north before acknowledging that which is above and that which is below.

We all cast the circle together. Sometimes, the circle is cast with an athame or sword, sometimes with a hand, and sometimes with drawing pentacles at each of the directions to help seal and strengthen. This circle holds the magick we will create.

Elements - Air, Fire, Water, Earth, Spirit

Once the circle is cast, we move to the elements, starting in the East with Air. We start at another point than where we started creating the circle for a number of reasons. (And there are likely more possibilities and interpretations.)

Some say we start the elements with Air because it is the East and the rising sun (Northern Hemisphere). Others say that we have different starting points for circle casting and elements because we are an offshoot of Feri and this was a way to bring in the Feri way of casting and following the elements.

What is consistent is the fact that we honor the elements after casting a circle, instead of doing both at the same time. I hold this has creating the magickal container first and then inviting the elements into that sacred space. I've also heard that this is a way to make sure both are given the reverence they deserve - without one being lost in the other.

Deity / Mysterious Ones

After grounding, casting, and elemental invocations, we move into the space that shifts depending on the work of the ritual.

Here are some of the beings we might honor or call in or acknowledge:

- The Fae
- Time
- Ancestors / Descendants
- Metaphors / Anthropomorphized Essences, e.g. labyrinth,

grief, passion
* Godds / Gods / Goddesses

This is not an all-inclusive list, and nor do we call all of these beings and essences all of the time. Based on the intention of the ritual and the work of the magick, we might call in some beings to support that work. It is true that we endeavor to call in beings who we will work with during the ritual, versus just calling them in without honoring them again in some way.

Tofu, a.k.a. The Meat of the Ritual

When I was teaching a class recently, someone asked how we do spells in ritual. Aren't all rituals spells? This answer is one that I've never said aloud, but it's true. In rituals, we create and build an intention, call in those to help us, do work to focus our intention and will, then build energy to boost that intention

Every ritual is a spell.

Perhaps the spell is different and it doesn't come with potions or chants. Perhaps the spell is subtle and personal. Perhaps the spell is quiet and long-term. But every ritual is a spell in some way. To help focus our intention and to get clarity, we might use various tools of discovery and engagement:

* Storytelling
* Pairs work
* Trance
* Stations
* Devotional Work
* Movement / Dance
* Improvisational ....

We'll go into these more in an upcoming section. The point of these practices is to allow ourselves the space to find out what we already know - and what we need to know. We can come together in these activities to explore our thoughts, our actions, and our interactions to inform future decisions and magick.

Energy Building

With the information we have gathered and the information that continues to emerge, we want to raise energy to give it life and power. We want to create energy together to strengthen our focus and our will and to increase the ability of our magick to deliver change.

We can raise energy in many ways: singing, chanting, dancing, and drumming. The key is to make sure the group as a whole comes together at the same time to focus on the same thing - the intention of the ritual. It may be that the words of the intention have faded, but all that we have learned is present and ready for liftoff.

In this moment, we also follow energy where it leads. Though often rituals will drive toward a loud singing and drumming moment where it becomes so loud that we can't hold the sound any longer and it rises up.....other rituals may not need that height. The energy might ebb and flow downward, or in a donut, or in some other form that allows the energy to go where it needs to go.

By being present in the energy, we allow the spell to charge up for what it does next. By having everyone together, we will do this work together.

Benediction

Once the energy building or raising or movement has ended, there is often a moment of silence. It is a moment that is purposeful, enabling the energy to settle and the magick to sit in the moment. After a period of time when the energy has settled, a priestess will give a benediction.

To put it simply, this is a piece where we remember what we

have done in ritual and how we hope it moves out in the world. It's the way to seal off the magick and bring us back to what we did after what is often an ecstatic energy piece. Together, we remember the spell. Together we move forward.

Food Blessing

To ground our bodies after magick, other traditions take cakes and ale after ritual. But we are a clean and sober tradition, so we do not use ale. We might bring juice and nuts or some other food item to share with each other. We will often say to another as we pass the food: May you never hunger. May you never thirst.

Devocations

As the food is passed around and people are coming back to their bodies, we will start to release and thank the energies that have gathered with us, in reverse order of their invocation.

These are times to bring in any last points or messages that might be helpful in moving out into the world. Finally, we open the circle and often will say something used in many traditions:

> May the circle be open, but unbroken, may the peace of the goddess/godds be ever in your hearts. Merry meet and merry part, and merry meet again.

Ritual Etiquette

If you're new to Reclaiming rituals, it can help to know what is expected of folks who participate and it can help you sink in more fully to the magick. Now that you have an understanding of what might happen in a ritual, here are some things you can keep in mind:

Participate at the level that feels good

We are a participatory tradition and we want you to feel welcome to do as guided in the ritual. And we understand if you're not sure what we're doing, you may not be comfortable. Participate as you like and as feels good. Know that your presence and your intention help the magick build.

Sing and move your body

The modern world likes to tell us that if we are not perfect in our offerings, we should not offer them. In Reclaiming (and to paraphrase Leonard Cohen): forget your perfect offering. Don't worry about how you sound when you sing or what your body looks like - you are beautiful and welcome.

Do not worry if you forget words to the song or you suddenly need to leave - it's fine. Just be aware of how your energy might impact the circle. If you have to leave, just seal up the circle after you, much like a curtain or a zippered door.

Maintain awareness of others

As with any new group, it can help to be aware of others and how your decisions might impact them. If you are called to move your arms around, feel free, but don't hurt someone who is standing next to you. If you want to close your eyes, feel free, and make sure you're not about to step on someone who is lying down.

Move slowly during the Spiral Dance, for example, as this will help everyone stay safe. The more you can sustain awareness, the more you will facilitate a safe experience for everyone. If people are in chairs, make sure you're not standing in front of them and blocking their view.

Ask for help if you need it

As mentioned before, graces and dragons are there to help. People who have identified themselves as ritualists can also help (given they're not in the middle of something else). If you need help getting a chair, ask. If you need help hearing, ask. If you need something to make you feel comfortable, ask.

Trust that your experience is valid

Sometimes you might go to a ritual and wonder if it 'did' anything. That's normal and expected. Instead of wondering if you did something right or if the ritual was right, it can help to release any attachment to explanation for about 24 hours. Sometimes magick needs a moment to settle into our bones. Once it has that chance, then you might understand what happened and how it impacted you. (And it's entirely possible the ritual wasn't what you needed right then!)

Ritual Technologies

In a Reclaiming ritual, many things can happen and emerge. There are things that are planned, things that are not, and things that occur that were perfectly imperfect. Some rituals require months of planning, others happen in the ten minutes before the door opens. For someone who is new to Reclaiming rituals, this can be very exciting and also different from other rituals. Though this is NOT an all-inclusive list of things that might happen in a Reclaiming ritual, it is a brief list of what you might encounter.

Trance

A commonly used tool in ritual is trance, or the exploration of the subconscious after being taken through an induction and journey to a place for discovery. This can happen with one voice leading the trance from start to finish, or it can involve multiple voices to layer in sound and words, while deepening the overall experience.

Milling

While some trances are experienced sitting or lying down, trances called milling trances are those which encourage movement as the body allows. You are encouraged to move around the ritual space, pondering questions. At some point, you are asked to slow down and find someone to share your answers with. You might do this sharing and then be asked to continue walking, coming back to new questions and new people to interact with.

Aspecting

Another ritual technology in Reclaiming rituals is aspecting. This is a practice of possession in which a priestess will open themselves up to the divine, take them in, and then interact in the world with the divine as the guide for their body and mind.

Aspecting can look like having someone draw the godd into the priestess or a priestess might put on an object that is imbued with the godd or the priestess will simply push out their consciousness to leave room for the godd to arrive.

Unlike other traditions, Reclaiming aspecting is not typically a full possession. It is taught that the body will always trump the spirit and that the priestess will always be able to release the deity when needed.

Aspecting is often used in rituals to give participants to a chance to hear the words of the godds or to ask questions of the godds. Sometimes the godds also want to have a chance to move around the world, explore it, and give messages to certain ritual participants.

In some rituals, participants might be asked to lightly aspect or to take on an item that is imbued with the godd's energy. This is a sacred act and not a party trick. The work of the priestess to embody the godd is a solemn responsibility and takes time to learn how to hold well.

Story and myth

There might also be Reclaiming rituals in which the participants get to embody or experience the story of the godds who are called. This can look like ritual drama, with multiple priestesses in roles, as well as movement around the ritual space to engage the audience.

This storytelling can help to inform a trance or it can help to bring the ritual into the space of the particular godds. In addition, this ritual drama can often help to pull people away from their own stories about the godds and enable them the chance to see other viewpoints. After all, you may begin to relate to a godd more when you see how they were impacted. Sometimes, stories and myths are a part of invocations as well, and sometimes participants will follow the story to a certain place and enter a trance to join the godds there.

Stations

When there are multiple ways to enter a story or there are multiple questions to be considered during a ritual, stations may be used. These are separate areas where a person can go and interact with another person or interact with an altar or be asked to interact with themselves in some way. For example, a person might go to a water altar that asks them to name what is holding them back and then cleanse themselves with water.

The stations can allow people to encounter the magick at their own pace, while being in community with others. These stations can also help to encourage layers of understanding to inform an energy building or a particular spell working.

Devotional Work

In addition, some rituals will offer a space for mystery to step in and guide what happens next. This might look like everyone coming up to an altar to interact with a certain deity or it might look like a dance or some sort of honoring.

For example, at one ritual, there is often a 'dressing' of a wooden framed dolly with flower and other greenery. This helps to invoke into the space and into the room the spirit of that goddess (often Brigid). In doing so, everyone who wants to participate can bring up a flower or bring something that will help to add to the devotion of this place.

It could also look like the entire group making nature-based art on the floor or a mosaic or an altar to a specific part of the wheel of the year. With everyone focused in the same energy and the same space, it brings into the ritual the energy of collaboration and of reverence. Perhaps, even communion with the godds, though not everyone might connect with that particular word.

* * *

Reclaiming ritual offers the opportunity to be fully immersed in your own personal work. It also offers you the opportunity to be in community with those who are looking for answers, just as much as you are.

What is important to remember is that these rituals are designed to not only challenge outdated or narrow thinking, but also to bring you into the place of trust and solidarity.

These magickal spaces allow us to remember (again and again) that we are not alone in this world. That we have the tools and the energy to keep going, no matter what our sacred cause or journey might be. We are not alone.

Chapter 6

Core Classes

It is said that to call yourself a Reclaiming Witch, you need only abide by the *Principles of Unity*. To go deeper into the tradition, however, it is advised that you move into the core classes to learn the basics of ritual in *Elements of Magic*, to engage with *Iron Pentacle*, to step into community with *Pearl Pentacle*, to uncover the story of yourself through dreams in *Rites of Passage*, and to gain skills of relationship amongst others in the *Communities Class*.

These classes each offer the groundwork of personal and communal engagement, the places where you can step even more fully into magick, activism, and knowing of self. Most often, you might take the classes in this order: *Elements of Magic*, *Iron Pentacle*, *Pearl Pentacle*, *Rites of Passage*, and the *Communities Class*. However, there are certainly witches who have taken them in a different order, revisited them at different points, and who have created another arc of experience.

What is true is that *Elements of Magic* is the place of beginning and of stepping into the magick of Reclaiming. It is often the prerequisite for other classes, and offers the foundation upon which other work is strengthened.

The Reclaiming Teaching Model

There could be long discussions about what a Reclaiming teacher is and how they should teach. What I will say is that the most commonly held belief is that everyone has wisdom to share. While there are students and there are teachers, classes are given ample space for group sharing and knowledge. In doing so, the magick becomes collaborative versus instructive.

While it's true that certain things are taught in classes and

49

are given as the foundational ideas of Reclaiming, there is room for expansion. Classes are often more experiential, enabling the opportunity for feeling into things to see what works best for you as a student (and, often, for you as a teacher and student).

Before we move forward, it is important to note that Reclaiming's value of non-hierarchy extends to how classes are formed and taught. Classes are taught with at least two teachers, in an effort to offer a model for shared power - and more sustainable work.

Teachers often go through a process of learning with other teachers in a student teacher role. This process can look like a student teacher teaching as many core classes with experienced (a.k.a. full) teachers as they can before moving into a full teacher role.

In the San Francisco CRAFT cell (the teacher's cell), there is a more specific process of applying to become a student teacher, then teaching with full teachers before applying to become a full teacher. The other teachers will discuss the person's skills, application, and any potential feedback that might help them grow and develop in their teaching roles.

Other Reclaiming communities without a teacher's cell may follow another process that allows student teachers to get the mentoring support they need to feel confident in their teaching ability for core classes.

Classes are offered on a sliding scale model, with the ability for those who can pay at the higher level to pay at that level and support those who might be at the lower end of the scale. That said, scholarships are available for most classes, with teachers being willing to find ways for everyone to take the class, no matter their income level.

The donations from the class will go toward supplies, space rental, advertising, and tithing back to Reclaiming. Teachers will often tithe back 7 - 10% to help support the website and other administrative tools available to all teachers.

The two teachers (and often a third or a student teacher) will actively work together to plan the class, what it looks like, what energies it might encounter, how it will be scheduled, etc. Some teachers might choose to offer classes in weekend formats (often called intensives or immersions), while others may choose six-week formats. And other formats have been created to hold the needs of students, communities, and the teachers themselves.

During classes, teachers will rotate roles of leadership, instruction, and participation. Since there is no one person who is considered to be in charge, the teachers act more as guides and holders of the container - so everyone can do the work that is calling for them.

While it's true each of the core classes has certain things to teach the students, this is not rigid or prescriptive. Instead, the classes are meant to bring people through a process of experiential learning in which they might uncover more about themselves, find answers to questions, and perhaps even decide to continue to work within the Reclaiming tradition.

Classes often involve individual work, small group work, and larger group work. Teachers will blend various learning methods to engage those who are visual, auditory, kinesthetic, and experiential learners, while also setting up containers for experience without attachment to outcome.

More often than not, classes emerge based on what happens between the unique folks who show up. Teachers will shift curriculum to meet the magick that arrives and the magick that demands to be witnessed.

Many times, classes become groups of people who end up creating covens or other witchy groups. And some classes end up working with other areas of Reclaiming, furthering connections and movement of magick.

Elements of Magic

As the first class most Reclaiming witches take, this is the place where we first come together, often from other traditions or different experiences of magic. This is the place where we explore the elements of Air, Fire, Water, Earth, and Spirit/ Center and relate to them with different aspects of Reclaiming as a tradition and practice. While each class is informed by the teachers who plan the class, there is a basic structure that looks like an exploration of each element:

Air

During this class, we will begin with the history of the tradition, the basic structure of ritual, the casting of a circle, and the use of consensus process to inform the way we relate to each other. In Reclaiming, we cast a circle by starting in the North (most often) and moving around the different directions, clockwise. We complete the circle before moving in to bring in all that is above and all that is below.

We call in the elements by starting in the East with Air, then South with Fire, then West with Water, North with Earth, and the Center with Spirit.

This class is often a class of conversation and getting to know each other. We begin to build a small community of witches and magick makers who are going on a journey together. What do we already know? What have we come to know? What are we learning?

We consider the idea of intention and how to form one that strengthens our magickal outcomes and potential. What do we want to do? What is the magick we are creating? We draw the line that aligns our mind with our action.

As we cast circles, we learn about holding energy in versus keeping energy outside. While circles are certainly protective and holding, they are also places where we are building magick so that when we open the circle again, it can pour out into the world.

In *Elements of Magic*, we will often work with visualization and holding an image in our minds so that it becomes something that forms into something more solid than a thought. We might hold the image of a bird that can fly with our wishes or we might do another spell working that enables us to know our mind as a tool of creation.

Fire

During the class on Fire, we work with energy and how to sense it. We practice the ways in which we already know energy and how we can build that skill to inform our magick. We touch energy, we feel energy, and we play with energy to understand how it interacts with us as much as we interact with it.

We begin to bring in opportunities to create the sacred space, using the energy we have to give on that day. And in this circle, we might meet each other, look at each other and sense into the energies we carry. We begin (or continue) the journey of trusting ourselves as energy. Perhaps we explore the energy centers of the body or we find words to describe the way we each, individually, feel into what is present.

With the knowledge of daring, we recognize and explore the way we can build energy for ritual. We speak of the cone of power and how it is the participation of all that creates force and momentum for spells.

The cone of power rises up when we are all sharing the intention we have named and we use different technologies to bring it into focus. We might sing, dance, chant, and/or drum to facilitate a connection between everyone. After all, when we're on the same page, we are mighty.

Energy is built by bringing everyone together, when our voices combine and we hold each other in this experience. We align our energies and they rise up, meeting in the apex of the cone (like a pointy hat) to shoot that energy out into the world. Our voices and our movements fuel the energy until it peaks into a wordless tone that rises and rises and rises. And at a moment, the tone dissipates and settles into silence.

The energy hums through our bodies and through the space. It is offered to the intention and then offered to the earth. A gift.

Water

The Water class is the class of trance and finding the place of power. It is building on what we know to bring us into the landscape of that space beyond our everyday knowing. This is the place of mystery and opening and travel between worlds.

We learn about trancework as it is used in Reclaiming. This is a journey that is not guided in the traditional sense, but more about guiding us to trust ourselves enough to find what we might find. Trancework in our tradition requires us to create a safe space for those who travel on the journey through an induction. We might relax our bodies and our minds by breathing and bringing our awareness to who we are - without trying to change or fix. We guide ourselves to trust and opening.

Trancework often uses techniques of hypnosis and NLP to deepen and create a starting point for a journey along a path. The path is not described as being a certain way, though it might have qualities to explore. Instead, the path is one that the person going on the trance will know when they get there because they are empowered to take this journey as only they know it.

The first trance might lead to the Place of Power (as outlined in 'The Spiral Dance'), a place where we feel fully ourselves and fully in our power. We will look in all directions to see what we see and know what we know. And all of our places of power will look different and will be shaped by our selves.

We might meet someone there, we might not. We might see or feel or sense things. We might meet a feeling or a quiet presence. All of the journeys are right and good and just as they might be.

From there, we will return the way we came, following the path we take, knowing we can always return to the place we have been. Often, the place of power becomes the place where you return when you have questions or you have other magickal work to do.

We offer the possibility that trancework can be open and inviting. We ask questions without offering answers. We suggest possibilities without offering concrete-ness. In Water, we trust the waves of our knowing.

Earth

With Earth, we explore the ways we are connected to the Earth itself, as well as the practice of spellwork. During this class, we might explore the depth of grounding before magickal work and we may create a spell together that will help solidify our intention from this point forward.

We might explore the activism as related to the Earth and our promise to be caretakers of the land. This has also become a place of traveling the land itself to reach out and know it as being not separate, but part of us.

In this class, we might return to the place of intention to bring our spellwork into focus. What do we want to bring into the world? What do we want to bring into our life?

We come together to learn and share knowledge of crafting spells. This is often the place where we might talk about correspondences and timing of spells. We might make spell pouches or create candles to focus our intentions. And using our knowledge of fire, we raise energy to bring our spells into reality.

Spirit/Center

Spirit (or Center) is the place of mystery and void and surrender. This is the element that swirls and knows and wonders. This is the place of cauldrons and stirring, while also being the place of divination.

We come together to seek wisdom. We might scry into dark water or mirrors. We might gaze into a fire while chanting to open up to what is making itself known. We might chant until the words fall away and all we can do is feel.

This might also be the time when we begin to think about what we want for our magickal lives moving forward. The class often uses the divination as the beginning of thinking about how to bring all of the information together to plan a ritual for the final class.

In this class, we might talk about how to construct a ritual, how to work together to create magick, and what is important when creating a ritual as a group.

But, again, every *Elements of Magic* class is different. So the magic that is here is just the starting point for what might arise, what might be conjured with a group of people who might never be in the same place at the same time ever again.

Iron Pentacle

Sometimes, Reclaiming is said to be an offshoot of Feri or a cousin or a line of the practice. While you might hear different thoughts from different Reclaiming witches, *Iron Pentacle* is a core class.

In this class, we explore the points of Sex, Pride, Self, Power, and Passion, moving around a pentacle starting at the top (Sex), moving down to the right foot (Pride), moving up to the left hand (Self), moving over to the right hand (Power), and back down to the left foot (Passion) before returning to the top of the head - as though the godds are painting the pentacle on us. And when the points are 'run,' then a clockwise circle is drawn around the points to close the circle - from Sex to Self to Passion to Pride to Power and then back to Sex.

"Iron is the work of this lifetime, while Pearl is the work of many lifetimes," as is often attributed to Victor Anderson. In Reclaiming, this is the work of knowing ourselves. It is the work of exploring, questioning, and challenging our own relationship with each of these points.

And, again, it is often informed by the teachers who plan the class and can be held in the context of myth or poetry or some other backbone as a flow for moving from point to point in each class or class section.

Often used as a tool of meditation and diagnosis, *Iron Pentacle* allows us to explore the shadows of us as humans. It is often said that this pentacle is the place of seeing where the overculture places certain limits or stories upon us. Or it is the place of looking at the ways in which we have placed definitions of these words onto our life experiences.

What is important to know about this class is that it is not an answering of questions or a decree of how things should be. After all, we are constantly in flux with the way we relate to ourselves. Instead, we are bringing awareness, within sacred space, to the places where we may feel out of balance with living fully in the world.

This Reclaiming class encourages vulnerability and honesty. We are encountering our own relationships with each point as they are now, knowing we can continue to explore and adjust. This class includes running the pentacle across our bodies, often as a shield or a settling to aid in difficult situations - or just to find where we are in the moment.

Iron Pentacle continuously offers us a way to step into our lives, running the energy of stars through our bodies, running the hot, red fire of iron to re-energize our weary and overwhelmed minds. In this earthy pentacle, we can tap into our birthright to live freely and fully.

Together may explore our sexual histories or the ways in which we navigate power. Or we might look at the ways in which we are in a strange relationship with pride or a confusion about what our 'self' really is.

Sex

Sex is the point of life force and sexuality and creation. It is often the place where we might become tangled in whether we are too sexual or not sexual enough - or something else. If we think about the ways in which Sex is stifled in much of culture, especially the United States and its Puritanical leanings, we can see how having this point out of balance can have an impact on our lives.

We explore our questions and beliefs about how we hold Sex in our lives. Where are we too much? Where are we too little? How do we come into a better relationship with this point?

This can be a vulnerable point in which we share parts of our sexual beings as we know them in this moment, and we might begin to expand our definition of what we consider to be our sexual identities.

Pride

In Pride, we traverse the question of right size in the world. How are we showing up fully and completely? How are we shrunken and hidden? Are we able to stand up and name the things we are proud of, much like a child would, without embarrassment or fear?

How do we step into living with the pride of who we are and what we have to offer? How do we name the things we are proud of and how can we ensure we do not fall into narcissism? How can we hold ourselves during times when we feel ashamed about who we are? How can we bring ourselves out of the spaces when we feel small?

This movement between the small and the too big becomes an exercise of finding what is right for us - and often finding out that we have been in one place for so long that heading to the place of right size feels uncomfortable.

Self

As we move into Self, we move into a place of definition and mystery. There is no one self that we can capture, as the self is often nebulous and shifting. After all, we are the same person we began after birth, but how we see ourselves has changed. How we act in the world has changed based on what we have learned, what we have experienced, and what we want to show up as.

So, Self becomes a point of checking what is true and what we might think is true. We might encounter masks or labels that don't quite fit us anymore. Or we might choose new labels to try on to see if they do fit.

We might need to gaze into a mirror long enough to let all of the possibilities fall away - and allow for something new and unexpected.

Power

Power is a point that can also show up in *Pearl Pentacle*, the power of how we relate in power with others - and with ourselves in *Iron Pentacle*. How do we hold power? How do we feel about power? Do we have stories about its positive and negative influences?

Do we know it as something that is scary? Do we know it in its ability to manipulate, sometimes for good?

This point can be a place where there are more questions than answers. In Reclaiming, we talk about Power-Over, Power-With, and Power-from-Within. Power-Over is the place of manipulation and trying to get someone else to do what you want them to do. Power-With is working with someone else to share power and to share resources.

Power-from-Within is self-empowerment, knowing what you have to bring and sharing that in service with others, but acting from your own grounded ability to hold power.

In this pentacle point, we start to question the places where we see Power-Over, where we see structures of oppression in the world, and where we challenge those in power. This class or class section can often be confronting as the various displays of power are uncovered.

We might begin to see the ways in which we are constantly

battling against those who would have power over us. What do we do? What can we do? How can we do things together? How have we been complicit? How can we step out of roles as the oppressor?

Passion

There are certainly ways in which the Passion point might seem to be simple. After all, it's just about what you want to do, isn't it? For some, this is the truth of their experience with this point. It's easy for some to name what they are passionate about, and they can talk for hours about what they love in the world.

But the Passion point is less about the what, and more about the drive. And some may find that drive to be less accessible or knowable. In some classes, the question is asked: What do you get up for in the morning? What would you do no matter what?

What is the thing that sings your song and knows your name? And how can you find that spark? How can you bring that closer to your reality and everyday life?

Remember, Passion is one of the points of the pentacle that holds the entire star up. It is a foundation and the point before returning to the beginning. What drives you home?

Pearl Pentacle

Some say that if you run *Iron Pentacle* enough times in your body, it will become pearly energy, that *Pearl Pentacle* emerges easily when the work of Iron is focused and steady. *Pearl Pentacle* is the work of how we relate to ourselves in community.

Moving around the body in the same way, the points are Love, Law, Knowledge/Wisdom, Liberty/Liberation/Power, and Wisdom/Knowledge. While *Iron Pentacle* points are often steady in how they are named, Pearl is watery.

Pearl Pentacle asks we engage with the bigger questions of what we bring into community. It asks us to become wider and open. As Victor Anderson notes, "Pearl is the work of many lifetimes."

This is big work, important work. Work that begins now and continues onward, with ramifications and lessons we might never see in our lifetime. But the more we engage, the more able we are to create the ripples that become waves in the future.

Love

"Love is the law, love under will." — Aleister Crowley, 'The Book of the Law.'

In Reclaiming, the myth of the Star Goddess finds its way into many classes and camps and rituals, as it is a creation myth that takes in both Feri gods and the proclamation of falling in love with one's self to birth new universes.

In *Pearl Pentacle*, in Reclaiming, this point is the beginning. It is the place of beauty and sometimes great heartbreak. Where is love in your community? Where has it grown and supported? Where has it faltered and struggled? Where has love shown up? What did you expect? What have you learned?

In love, we encounter not only the places of interaction among our communities, but also the stories of love that have brought us to this particular point. Can we look at our love as being a practice of coming back or returning? Can we seek to know and love ourselves so much that we surrender to great mysteries? Can we find love and heal our relationship to love so that we might serve each other well?

Law

From Love, we move to Law, a place of structure and rigidity. We move into a place where we know things are being defined and expected. But we also encounter real issues with the way law has also oppressed and hurt.

Often, in Reclaiming, this point moves into a conversation of the laws of nature and how things work to support each other. Sometimes, we also talk about the laws we hold for our own selves, how they serve and how they don't.

We might also look to laws in society, the laws that seek to protect us (e.g. the agreement that we all stop at traffic lights) and the laws that are not enforced fairly (e.g. more arrests of persons of color).

Knowledge / Wisdom

In Reclaiming, the *Pearl Pentacle* can vary. And, truthfully, this pentacle might shift each time you see it in class, as many teachers and students hold it in different ways. As mentioned before, you are your own spiritual authority, so you may need to run this pentacle a few times to see what works best for you.

That said, Knowledge can often come next and can be associated with what we know to be true. This might include facts and figures or unique talents we hold. What does this knowledge bring to community? What can knowledge offer that serves?

And conversely, what is the shadow side of knowledge? How do we separate knowledge from alternative facts or propaganda? How do we stay clear in the way we accept things to be true? How do we find information and how do we let outdated or incorrect knowledge go?

Liberty / Liberation / Power

Moving along in the *Pearl Pentacle*, we come to Liberty or Liberation (and sometimes Power). This point shifts depending on the class and the teachers, and most often lands on Liberty or Liberation, asking the question of what it means to be truly free.

What does it mean to liberate and be free in community? What does it mean to encounter the places of stuckness or confusion or limitation? How do we find and live our definition of liberation without impacting others negatively?

And that is why Power becomes another possibility for this pentacle point. We can also look at this point as a point speaks to the idea of being one's own spiritual authority in community.

Wisdom / Knowledge

Wisdom is discussed as being the place where you have the knowledge and you know what to do with it. You have taken time or energy to integrate the things you know and you can shift from knowing into doing. Some say this is a place where you are in action. Others might say that wisdom comes from trusting yourself in community. Wisdom is also inherent, without needing to be preceded by knowledge gathering. And still others might say that wisdom comes from connecting with the divine for their wisdom. Or all of the above - and more.

Rites of Passage

Rites of Passage is a class that seems to be the 'final' class in the core classes. It's often the class that people end on before heading out to do other things in the Reclaiming community besides taking classes for a while.

From the name, it would appear to be a class that teaches you about rites of passage, how to do them, and how to create them. And while this is a part of the idea, the class is more about the ideas of dreamwork and rewriting your story as tools of initiating yourself into a new self.

But that's a little vague, isn't it? Often, this class does use a story to help guide students through the places of encountering dreams and seeing their wisdom. Working closely with each other, the class often shares dreams, acts them out, and offers each other insights based on their observations.

This is also often a class in which a student might be asked to write out the story of their life, but not as a step-by-step narrative. They might be asked to look at their life as a fairy tale and they are the hero or hera. In that lens, what would their story look like? How would it sound? What does their story inspire?

The stories are often shared and performed and brought into

being, often bringing people to a threshold of understanding - that their story is still being written.

Some classes will talk about the process of initiation in Reclaiming, and fold in the general steps of an initiatory process as part of the class outline. This enables folks to hear about this practice and to begin to understand what it might look like - or at least whether it's something they'd like to pursue in the future.

This class is mysterious and ever-changing. It offers places of trance work and group work and ritual, places where the unexpected occurs. And while it is not a class of initiation, it is often very initiatory.

Communities

More recently, the *Communities Class* has become part of the core class lineup. Though created and consensed on in 2012 at a Dandelion gathering, it is only recently being taught on a more frequent basis.

While *Pearl Pentacle* is a class of how we relate to community, the *Communities Class* is the class of learning skills to work in community. We might work with consensus, conflict resolution, communication, ritual planning, and service. This class offers a wide and long list of curriculum goals for those who are brand-new to Reclaiming or for those who have been around the community for a while.

During this class, there are ways to approach the work through the elements, through pentacles, and through other formats that move naturally to encourage group participation. Often, this class will bring together people from many Reclaiming communities, fostering conversations about privilege, the *Principles of Unity*, anti-oppression work, transgender support, and all of the things that have come up in that present moment.

The *Communities Class* is one that I hold with great care and responsibility - as I do all of the core classes. But the first time I taught this, I felt myself become nervous about how I was holding the material. I wanted to talk about the ways in which Reclaiming has been wonderful - and I also wanted to offer space for ongoing conversations about ways in which we need to work more on trans, POC, class, and accessibility issues.

There is space for hard conversations, to be sure, in this class. And while I'm not sure we were able to come up with any solutions just yet, the honest dialogue is hopeful - and made me proud of my tradition.

* * *

It's true, this section on classes is long and detailed because the classes are the core foundation of Reclaiming as a tradition. While there are books about Reclaiming readily available (and listed in the Appendix), the experience of magick in community is ideal for finding out how Reclaiming magick works with your magickal needs. Being in community is part of the magick, meeting people is part of the mystery, what you will uncover together is part of the joy.

Chapter 7

Witchcamps around the World

To some, Witchcamp sounds like a Harry Potter fantasy come true. And while there is magick to be made at these camps, Reclaiming offers them more as intensive opportunities for deep work and deep magick.

These are not festivals, in the sense that many might know that word. Instead, Witchcamps in Reclaiming are the place where people can come together, build a highly supportive community, dive into myth and magick, and come out of the experience changed.

Why Witchcamp?

Once upon a time, the first Reclaiming Witchcamp was held near Mendocino, California, USA at a place called Jug Handle Creek. When you ask people when that first camp took place, you might get different answers, but the general consensus is that it took place in the 1980s. From that experience came other camps in British Columbia and California.

Witchcamp is a time to get away from the world, to step out of the everyday pressures of life and step into the places of liminal. By being able to create a community, much as Burning Man, of people who share the same ideas or passions, you create a place of safety for exploration of deeper questions.

Many people who go to Witchcamp will offer it as the place where their life changed. Without access to (or encouraged disengagement with) mobile phones and internet, the mind can detach from noise. By reconnecting with nature, often deep in the forests or far away from cities, Witchcamp returns us to the knowing that comes from the Earth.

The decision to go to Witchcamp is a personal one, one that

might be informed by spiritual questions or curiosities. It can also be a decision to see people who you might not see the rest of the year, a homecoming of sorts.

Or Witchcamp can be the place to immerse yourself fully in magick and community. (A short personal story - my first experience of Reclaiming outside of reading 'The Spiral Dance' was going to a Witchcamp. It did change my life and changed the course of my magickal practice.)

What Witchcamp Offers

Each Witchcamp is different. Each camp is informed and influenced by the land upon which it rests and the community that helps with organization. What is most common about witchcamps is that they include:

- **Immersion in nature** - Most camps are situated in wild areas, some with rustic camping and some with cabins, some with more facilities and some with less. What is consistent is that there is access to wild places so one can get lost, sometimes literally, but more often metaphorically. The closeness with nature allows for healing and connection and reconnection.

- **Daily classes** - Each morning, there are classes called paths offered by teachers on the teaching team. These classes are inspired by a story or theme of the camp, and they will take place most days during camp for around three hours. Sometimes they are held outside and sometimes not, sometimes they offer certain skill sets and some offer invitations into self-exploration and encountering personal shadows. The content varies widely and campers are encouraged to listen to their intuition when choosing the path they will take for the entirety of camp.

- **Nightly rituals** - Camps will offer nighttime rituals, and some daytime ones, that go even deeper into the story or myth of the camp. These rituals are ecstatic, participatory, and often edge-pushing. Rituals can be many hours long, around a fire, and include everything from sacred space and trance to journeys into the wild and ecstatic dancing or shapeshifting. There are often drums and energy building and sweaty witches.

- **Optional Offerings** - During afternoons at camps, campers can offer optional offerings to others. These are times for discussions, additional workshops, walks, potion making, etc. Any camper can sign up for these within the available time slots and locations.
- **Affinity Groups** - At the start of most camps is the chance to get into an affinity group. These are groups that can be self-selected or they can be selected based on picking up items and then finding others that have those items. Every afternoon, these groups meet to check-in about their camp experiences and get support. In some camps, affinity groups will have a chance to plan and execute a ritual on their own to foster even more intimacy.
- **Nourishment** - Magickal work (especially at this intensity) requires nourishing food and times for rest. Witchcamps endeavor to give campers all of the nutrition they can, while managing the vast needs of those with certain medical or ethical concerns.
- **Safety** - Because the camps are secluded and the communities agree to certain rules ahead of time, a camper can easily immerse in the magickal experience. They are surrounded by people who are just as committed to their spiritual development as they are, and who are committed to confidentiality, practiced in consent culture, and supporting of the POU.
- **Support** - Witchcamps are also a place where people can be supported in the places they need to go as part of their spiritual journey. With affinity groups and a culture that

accepts all gender histories, expressions, and shifts, as well as sexualities, pronouns, class backgrounds, cultures, races, and more, there is a place for everyone to find support. While it's certainly true that support continues to be examined for areas of internalized sexism, racism, and transphobia, the community attempts to support all who participate.

- **Accessibility** - Some of the camps are more rugged than others, and there are ways in which campers who need physical support will be provided a buddy or a more accessible living arrangement. In addition, those who might need help around vision or hearing or other medical conditions are supported as best as the camp and its organizers can.

- **Financial accessibility** - Because of the awareness around class and financial disparity, Witchcamps strive to offer scholarships so that all who might want to attend can attend. Some camps will also offer early registration and discounts for certain groups, including persons of color. At the time of writing this, Winter Witchcamp was able to offer a Pay-What-You-Can model, enabling those who were unable to pay the opportunity to go to camp.

While Witchcamps do happen in a community, with up to 120 people in a camp for up to a week, there are many personal benefits to attending. Each person will walk away with an experience that they will hold in their hearts, and an experience that might shape the way they live their lives from the moment camp ends.

Adults / All Ages Camps

In response to campers who wanted to have a camp experience with their children - or without - all ages camps have emerged as possible magickal experiences. Witchlets in the Woods and

Redwood Magic camps in California are considered family camps, and CloudCatcher in Australia, Vermont Camp in Vermont, USA, and DragonRise in the UK are considered all-age camps. These camps allow families to attend together, with paths for all ages and for adults. There is also a 'teen' camp that supports campers between the ages of 13 and 25.

Camps for all ages will offer rituals that support both adults and younger campers, while also helping to create community across ages. These camps are often restorative for adults as childcare is shared in community and there is space for everyone to have a personal magickal experience.

How to Choose a Witchcamp

To get a better sense of the Witchcamps, it can help to visit websites and Facebook pages that give more details. Some camps have mailing lists and other opportunities to connect so you can see what the cultures look like and how they might fit your spiritual needs.

- **Ask questions** - Talk to the organizer(s) of the camps to ask questions that are important to you. Be willing to be vulnerable about your needs and your limitations or any concerns you might have.
- **Talk to campers** - It can also help to talk to folks who have gone to the camp in the past. People love to share stories of their experiences, which can help you assess if that camp is a good fit.
- **Attend a public ritual in the area** - When you're able, you may want to attend a ritual that's near the camp as that will often include folks who are involved in camp planning.
- **Take a class with a camp teacher** - Or you can look at previous camps to see who the teachers were and take a class with one of the teachers to get a feel for what they might bring to a camp, though a class and camp are often

very different in scope and don't share the same context.

Even if I did describe what a Witchcamp included, it's hard to convey the magick and the intensity in words. Sometimes, you just have to go to know if you've made the right decision. And not everyone goes to Witchcamps. Or some people just go to Witchcamps. There's magick for everyone.

North America
Aurora Borealis Witchcamp, Central Alberta, Canada
British Columbia Witchcamp, Vancouver, British Columbia, Canada
California Witchcamp, Mendocino Woodlands, California, USA
Free Cascadia Witchcamp, USA
Mysteries of Samhain, Mendocino Woodlands, CA, USA
Redwood Magic, Mendocino Woodlands, CA, USA
Spiralheart Witchcamp, Four Quarters Interfaith Sanctuary, Artemas, PA, USA
Teen Earth Magic, Mariposa Institute, Ukiah, CA, USA
Tejas Witchcamp, Central Texas, USA
Vermont Witch Camp, Plymouth, VT, USA
Wild Ginger Witchcamp, Honeywood, Ontario, Canada
Wild Maine Witchcamp, Tenants Harbor, ME, USA
Winter Witchcamp, Northern Minnesota, USA
Witchlets in the Woods, Mendocino Woodlands, CA, USA

Europe
DragonRise Witchcamp, Wildways on the Borle, Shropshire, UK
Litha Camp, Tierra de Gredos, España
Phoenix Witchcamp, Oldenbütte, Germany

Australia

CloudCatcher Witchcamp, Springbrook Plateau, Queensland, Australia

EarthSong Witchcamp, Victoria, Australia

Chapter 8

Across the Generations

Reclaiming Witchcraft as a tradition has been around since the 1980s, which means it is still a younger tradition, in the eyes of some. This also means we have a wide spectrum of ages in our tradition, which we hope to hold well as we evolve. We have folx who have been with us since the beginning, and those who have passed on. We have those who have been born into this tradition, and those who have grown up as Witches alongside their parents.

We have couples who have come together and fallen apart. We have folks who have explored their gender and sexual orientation and identities and ways of relating. And we welcome into our tradition all of the ways that we engage in the life stages.

But in these varying stages and growth and emergence comes the greater questions of how we celebrate the wisdom across all ages - and how we ensure ongoing visibility and support for those who have already given so much to the tradition.

The Support of Elders

As we continue to pass through the years, Reclaiming has noted and started to bring into focus the way we interact with those we call elders (though they may not take on that mantle just yet). Because of the way that we plan and schedule classes and camps, for example, there are ways in which the energy needed to hold those roles is often more available in younger teachers and organizers.

While various Reclaiming communities have different approaches to how elders might be supported and recognized in communities (at least those who want to be recognized), here are some ways in which we are attempting to bring attention to our beloveds.

- Taking responsibility for ways in which Elders have not been supported well
- Asking for input about what Elders want from the community and how we may have failed them
- Listening to the answers without defensiveness or argument
- Identifying specific roles that might help them share their unique wisdom or gifts
- Involving Elders in all available roles for rituals, teaching, camps, presentations, etc.
- Telling stories of Elders who have passed on or those who have stepped away

In my own experience, I know there are ongoing conversations too about how we might support those Elders who are older and may not be well. Can we find ways to aid them in times of medical crises, for example? Are we able to reach out effectively and have resources available when they need support?

The Exploration of Experience & Innovation
One of the ways that generations have found themselves coming together for conversations around magick is the discussion of experience vs. innovation. Another way to put this is the discussion of whether we need to change things in order to make them better, or if the 'old' ways are just as good.

There have been conversations around Reclaiming about what happens when things aren't done as they have been in the past. Keeping in mind the idea of 'one's own spiritual authority in community,' it's unsurprising that things have happened in rituals and classes that look different from how those ritualists and teachers were taught.

For example, in the book 'Elements of Magick' that was

compiled by two Reclaiming teachers and featured many more teachers and ritualists, this book shows the various ways that each teacher approaches teaching the *Elements of Magick*, class. Some of the exercises were reshaped by the various voices in the book, and they look similar to the original exercises...but they are different.

In an ever-evolving tradition, there is a question about whether things need to change or if they should remain the same. And I don't think I can answer it. What I can say is that this conversation is one that seems to fall across generational lines of the tradition, with the 'younger' folx wanting to change things up.

I leave this quandary here to continue to be something that is discussed and to be reflected upon as you, the reader, continue to learn more about Reclaiming and its connection to you.

Bringing up Children

There generations of Reclaiming also brought into the tradition children of all stories and expressions. With these children came new questions about how we hold each other in community. How do we support new parents and if we are not, how can we do that better?

In the current time of the writing of this book, there are certainly places for families in Reclaiming, as all ages are typically welcome at most rituals. (Samhain/Spiral Dance can sometimes be boring for kids!) And there are family and teen camps that help offer spaces of being in magickal spaces with your peers.

But it has to be noted that there are ways in which parents need more support. After all, parents don't want to stop their own spiritual practice or give up the way it looked before parenting. They want to go to 'adult' rituals and camps to get their spiritual recharge. However, not all camps and classes and rituals have the space for children to be there. Thus, there are more ritual spaces that are opening up to the possibility of a children's corner or activity during the working for adults. This way, everyone can celebrate that day's magick.

Some of the Witchcamps are beginning to welcome all ages so that families can come together. There are paths that are designed to support all ages with teachers who have worked with all ages in the past.

In addition, it's not just babies and toddlers who need more support, it is also those children who are transitioning into the space of not being a toddler but not being a teenager. And then those who are a teenager or almost-teenager or those who are not a teenager anymore.

All of these overlapping and crisscrossing areas of community have generated questions about rites of passage for the different groups. While some camps will have age-specific paths and groups to help bring people together by age, those that don't or those Witches who don't feel they fit into certain groups can feel left out.

Because Reclaiming does continuously look at the ways that we are supporting each other - and how we are not - these conversations continue. These transitions and groups continue to be heard and asked for input on opportunities to support.

Chapter 9

Magickal Activism

Our beginnings in political activism are well-documented in pictures, stories, and books from various Reclaiming authors and participants. From the WTO to the G8 to marches on Washington and in the streets of San Francisco and around the world, as well as smaller actions, Reclaiming has active Witches who will put themselves in challenging situations (physically and emotionally) to protect people and the Earth.

Where Activism's Influence Shows Up

What you may have noticed in the history of Reclaiming is that the overall movement toward being more organized came from the actual protest and activist work. The more tools the groups learned to bring people together in solidarity, the more those tools showed up as important in magickal groups and ritual planning.

Consensus Decision-Making

At several points of this book, there has been a mention of 'consensus' as the way in which decisions are made in Reclaiming.

"We make decisions by consensus, and balance individual autonomy with social responsibility." - Principles of Unity

The movement behind consensus is to allow for everyone to have an opportunity to speak and to create a container in which everyone can feel good about the decision in the end. To come to 'consensus' is to come to an agreement with everyone being on board, knowing full well that not everyone will be in 100% agreement, but the final decision is the best for community.

Consensus process is held within group settings by, first, everyone agreeing to that structure of decision-making. After that, meetings that use consensus will start by having several roles at the minimum:

1. Facilitator
2. Note taker / scribe
3. Timekeeper
4. Vibes watcher

The Facilitator is the person that makes sure the meeting continues to move forward toward the goal of decision making. They are the ones who are leading the conversations, but not the actual decisions. They will make sure that conversations do not go off track, that everyone is being heard, and that decisions get clear consensus (a.k.a. everyone agrees). The facilitator often (not always) will call on those with hands up and take a stack (list) of those who have suggested they have something to say.

The Note taker or scribe does exactly what it sounds like - they take notes to ensure the discussions are being recorded in some way and that the Facilitator does not have to write things down as they watch the conversations move forward.

The Timekeeper will watch the time as agreed to by the group. They will let the group know when they have reached certain points of time and how much time is left in a discussion item.

The Vibes watcher may not always be present, but they are a role that can help everyone notice when things feel sticky or in need of attention. They might point out that someone seems upset or that someone is not as engaged as they were at one point. This can help to bring attention to something the facilitator or other group members may not have attended to well. With this knowledge, things can be resolved and things can be settled before moving into decision-making.

The rules of engagement include not speaking over another person; only taking up the space that is necessary, leaving room for everyone to talk; focusing on saying something new vs. repeating what has already been said; putting the needs of the community before personal agendas; maintaining respect and concern for each other; and adhering to agreements for time.

Each meeting requires an agenda of items to be discussed, often collected ahead of time. This list can be short or long, depending on the needs of the group. What is clear is that the time container of the meeting will only be able to cover what items can be covered. At the start of the meeting, the facilitator and the group may decide together how much time to allot to each agenda item, and then follow those time containers unless they choose to go over as a group.

From there, the meeting moves forward, agenda item by item. These items might be placed for discussion or they might be places for decision-making. In a discussion point, the group will talk and share ideas or information. Often, these agenda items are long-term ideas or things without a clear timeframe.

When it comes to places for decision-making, this might begin with a conversation about something that needs to be done. People continue to talk until someone feels they can craft a proposal for the group to decide upon. The proposal might get an immediate agreement for consensus or it might need some friendly amendments. This part of the process can take a few moments to complete, and it's wise to remember the more voices you heard, the more likely it is that the decision is one that works best for everyone.

With all of this said, consensus sometimes gets a bad reputation. It is thought to be difficult, time-consuming and complicated. This is true - and so is the work of community. With different voices and different ideas, it can take time to come to a decision that works for every single person.

This is why it's good to stop and take a breath. It is wise to tone down the energy of the room and stop a conversation if things need to breathe for a moment. It can also be wise to learn facilitation tools that can help see where questions need to be asked or to see where ideas have not been fully heard.

Some tools include:

- Stopping the conversation for a break - Having folks step back in order to collect their thoughts often helps create clarity.
- Straw poll - Ask the group to use thumbs up or down to show their agreement with a certain decision or proposal. Folx can also use a thumbs in the middle of they have no strong feelings in either direction.
- Fish bowl - Position the two people with the most opposite views on a decision in the center of the room. Invite them to have a conversation in front of everyone else so the group can see what they feel.
- Spectrum - Invite the group to stand in a line with each decision at the opposite end. People who agree more with one point will stand closer to that point, while those who do not might go to the other end, or stand in the middle.
- Charettes - These are smaller sub-groups of the larger group that might be empowered to have their own discussions and make decisions. These might include those who are fully invested in a certain part of ritual, for example, and they come back to the larger group with their decision.

What you're doing with these tools is to see where folks are not quite on board with a decision. Instead of looking at the group who is in agreement with what is being said, you open up the conversation to be with the people who are still not sure or who have issues.

In consensus, you need to address those questions and those issues as a group. This might be as simple as someone having their concerns heard or it might require the proposal to be changed completely.

If there is a decision that cannot be agreed to, a person might choose to block. This is the thing many people have heard of in groups that use consensus, and it sounds scary. And yes, in some spaces, it is a tool that can be used to promote an agenda instead of stopping something that needs to be stopped.

A block is a tool that one should only use if the decision might be harmful, unsafe, unethical, or out of bounds with the POU, for example. Thus, the block should not be used if you don't want a certain kind of flower at a ritual, but it might be wise if the ritual plan seems to include something that could burn the building down on purpose.

Once a decision is made and folx have consensed on it, then the decision is set and is followed by the group. If the decision does not make sense in the future, the group needs to come together again to have a new discussion, agree to rewrite or replace the previous decision, and then consense on that new decision.

The consensus process is used during ritual planning, organizing, and other meetings to bring people together, to bring voices together, and continue the work that we are charged with - holding community, our values, and the way we want to make magick in the world.

Affinity Groups

Another influence of activism is the use of affinity groups. These are small groups of people with shared interests who support each other in their common goals. Affinity groups are used in activist groups to bring personal feelings to the surface for discussion and support. These are often found at Witchcamps to offer people a place to be vulnerable and held in their experiences. You might share your experiences, holding confidentiality and ensuring people do not feel alone as they move into their power or into a role.

For example, at a Witchcamp, these groups can be chosen by different objects that people pick and then they find the people with the same items. Or the groups might be self-selected by people who want to affin (as we call it) together. Or groups might be based on certain interests (e.g. photography, nature walks, drumming). Or the groups might be comprised of people who identify as POC (persons of color) or gender histories. They then meet every day for a certain period of time to check-in about their camp experience. These affinity groups can also be tasked with creating their own rituals during the course of camp as an act of solidarity and camaraderie.

Many people find that their affinity groups can extend beyond camps and classes into circle and covens who gather for years after since they already have a solid foundation of experience.

The Personal is Political

What might be important to say is that while larger political actions will often get the most visibility, activism can show up in other ways. Activism can also look personal work that then influences others around you. For example, you might focus on the work of being a parent or of being a person who actively seeks out ways to reduce consumption or dismantle capitalism.

Instead of being defined by activism looking a certain way, Reclaiming offers opportunities for everyone to get involved in the level they can. After all, an activist who has physical challenges or limited resources cannot always put themselves into situations where they might be arrested or harmed.

People may choose to speak up for those without voices. They might choose to point out situations of racism or violence toward the trans community. One might make sure to share knowledge of how to do consensus in groups or how to navigate complicated legal situations.

There is activism for everyone - of all abilities and of all motivations. When something is personal to you, it is likely to feel personal for someone else too.

How People Can Get Involved

There are multiple ways to get involved in activism in Reclaiming, depending on what you are interested in and what you are drawn to. The best way to find your people, so to speak, is to share your ideas and your passions. Find a way to create a group, having meetings, and come up with ways to enact your activism in the world.

You might show up to a ritual planning cell with the idea of bringing activism into the ritual planning and workings. You might join a discussion about anti-racism efforts or organize training with local groups to learn what is most needed in their work.

You can show up at protests, at educational gatherings for local indigenous groups, and find you own way to take action. While Reclaiming is wide and its community broad, there are many ways to bring your own flavor of activism to the world.

Start a group

- Join up with another group
- Ask those who you respect what they do and how you can help
- Educate yourself about local issues and actions
- Get training in consensus
- Attend protests and actions
- Share events and information with others
- Make everyday decisions that support what you want to help in the world
- Be willing to make mistakes before you make changes
- Be willing to show up again and again

Know that the 'smallest' of actions can inspire others to do something to influence change. And while you may only be one person, you are in a community that is collaboratively inspired and eager to have you join the work of this time.

This doesn't mean you need to do everything or that you need to take on all of the challenges of the world. But what it does mean is that whatever calls you the most to take a step, take that step.

Conclusion

Reclaiming is an ever-evolving and ever-inspired tradition. With roots in goddess spirituality, feminism, activism, and politics, this is a community that actively seeks to blend magick with action. With the *Principles of Unity* at the foundation and a myriad of community members, this is a witchcraft tradition that does not seek to separate the 'everyday' from the magickal. We all have a place in the magick. We all have a place in the moving forward.

This is not to say that Reclaiming is some infallible or perfect tradition. This is not to say that we don't make mistakes or that we think differently than we did years or decades ago. This is not to say that we won't change again as we learn more and as we make mistakes.

I cannot tell you where we are headed, but I can tell you that I want to head in that direction. I cannot tell you that I agree with everything that everyone does, but that's a part of the growing and the potential.

To me, Reclaiming offers the reminder that the world shifts and changes, no matter what we do. But it also shifts and changes because of what we do. While the moon might shine and hide, while the light might grow and fade, we can rise together to join hands in the magick of what is becoming.

We can come together to hear the hurting hearts and the ways we have not done the best we could. We can listen harder and we can be quiet more often. We can speak when things need to be said, and we can step back to ensure all voices have a place.

I hold in my heart a vision of the world as a place of collaboration and magick. A place where we are not separate people, but where our uniqueness and our histories enable us to be better - together. I hold in my heart the possibility of safety for all bodies, especially for black and brown and trans bodies.

We have changed and we will change again. We are reclaiming ourselves as much as we are reclaiming power and magick. We are a tradition whose history began as a response to all those things around us, and we will continue to rise up to meet whatever comes next.

* * *

And to close this magick for today, for this moment, we give thanks to the allies, the godds, the ancestors and the descendants, the beings who walk with us and whose stories and myths inspire us to action. These beings are sacred. We give thanks to the elements of Center/Spirit, Water, Fire, Air, and Earth. All of these elements are sacred. We open the circle that has held us in our explorations and our questions. This circle is sacred.

We open the circle to release our empowered selves into the world.

Thank you to those who have come before. Thank you to those who will come next. Thank you to those who are here.

Merry meet and merry part. And merry meet again.

Appendix A: Ritual Planning & Outline

To help create ease in ritual planning, it can help to plan by following the elements that we invoke:

CENTER - What is the transformation we seek to create in this ritual? What is the magick?

AIR - What is the intention of the ritual? What is the story we will tell?

FIRE - What is the energy of the ritual? What is the structure of the energy? What might be needed to create it?

WATER - What are the emotions of this ritual? What is the flow? What is under the surface?

EARTH - What logistics do we need to keep in mind? What props/supplies do we need? How will we get from that point to the other point?

It can help to move through these steps, perhaps in an order that makes sense to your group, or perhaps in this order as a starting point.

Here are some other ideas to help with brainstorming on your own or in a group:

- What are we doing? Why are we doing it?
- Talk about the moon and the energetic placement of the day; the sabbat.
- Intention creation: brainstorming; dropped and open; thinking about the holiday/date; deities; energy from a

previous ritual that might be carried forward; what's at stake?

- What will serve this work? How will we move toward fueling the energy for the intention?
- Do we need introspection? Group/partner work?
- How can we all move into the liminal space to make magick together?
- Assigning roles – how does each role serve the intention? Who will take on this role? One person? Multiple persons?
- What songs/chants/dance leader(s) do we need?
- Drumming and music - who can support this role? How many people do we need? Who will guide the energy and follow the intention of the ritual as well as align with the energy of the group as it emerges?
- What do we need to bring/make/do?

BASIC RITUAL OUTLINE

Intention	
Cleansing	
Grounding	
Casting	
Elements	
Allies/Time/Archetypes	
Ancestors/Descendants	
Deity/Deities	

Working (trance, meditation, stations, story, something else!)
Energy Building
Benediction
Food Blessing
Devocations
What to bring & do
Songs/Chants/Dance Leader(s)

Appendix B: Resources

Listed below are books with more information about Reclaiming Witchcraft magick and the practices taught in classes, the activism seen on the streets, etc.

Diane Baker
- Circle Round: Raising Children in Goddess Traditions – with Anne Hill & Starhawk

T. Thorn Coyle
- Evolutionary Witchcraft (advanced workings)
- Kissing the Limitless

Luke Hauser
- Direct Action: An Historical Novel – activist back-story of Reclaiming (free download)
- Teen Earth Magic: An Empowerment Workbook (free download)

Jane Meredith & Gede Parma
- Magic of the Iron Pentacle
- Elements of Magic – editors – plus many Reclaiming contributors!

M. Macha NightMare
- Pagan Pride: Earth & Goddess
- The Pagan Book of Living & Dying – with Starhawk

Jone Salomonsen
- Enchanted Feminism: Ritual, Gender, and Divinity among the Reclaiming Witches of San Francisco

Starhawk
- The Spiral Dance: A Rebirth of the Ancient Religion of the Goddess
- Dreaming the Dark: Magic, Sex, & Politics
- Truth or Dare
- The Earth Path
- The Empowerment Manual: A Guide for Collaborative Groups
- The Twelve Wild Swans: A Journey to the Realm of Magic, Healing, and Action
- The Last Wild Witch
- The Fifth Sacred Thing
- Walking to Mercury
- City of Refuge
- Circle Round: Raising Children in Goddess Traditions – with Anne Hill & Diane Baker
- The Pagan Book of Living & Dying – with M. Macha NightMare

Online Resources:
www.Reclaiming.org
www.ReclaimingQuarterly.org
www.Starhawk.org
www.Witchcamp.org

MOON
BOOKS

PAGANISM & SHAMANISM

What is Paganism? A religion, a spirituality, an alternative
belief system, nature worship? You can find support for all these
definitions (and many more) in dictionaries, encyclopaedias, and
text books of religion, but subscribe to any one and the truth will
evade you. Above all Paganism is a creative pursuit, an encounter
with reality, an exploration of meaning and an expression of the
soul. Druids, Heathens, Wiccans and others, all contribute their
insights and literary riches to the Pagan tradition. Moon Books
invites you to begin or to deepen your own encounter, right here,
right now.
If you have enjoyed this book, why not tell other readers by
posting a review on your preferred book site.

Recent bestsellers from Moon Books are:

Journey to the Dark Goddess
How to Return to Your Soul
Jane Meredith
Discover the powerful secrets of the Dark Goddess and
transform your depression, grief and pain into healing
and integration.
Paperback: 978-1-84694-677-6 ebook: 978-1-78099-223-5

Shamanic Reiki
Expanded Ways of Working with Universal Life Force Energy
Llyn Roberts, Robert Levy
Shamanism and Reiki are each powerful ways of healing; together,
their power multiplies. *Shamanic Reiki* introduces techniques to
help healers and Reiki practitioners tap ancient healing wisdom.
Paperback: 978-1-84694-037-8 ebook: 978-1-84694-650-9

Pagan Portals – The Awen Alone
Walking the Path of the Solitary Druid
Joanna van der Hoeven
An introductory guide for the solitary Druid, *The Awen Alone* will
accompany you as you explore, and seek out your own place
within the natural world.
Paperback: 978-1-78279-547-6 ebook: 978-1-78279-546-9

A Kitchen Witch's World of Magical Herbs & Plants
Rachel Patterson
A journey into the magical world of herbs and plants, filled with
magical uses, folklore, history and practical magic. By popular
writer, blogger and kitchen witch, Tansy Firedragon.
Paperback: 978-1-78279-621-3 ebook: 978-1-78279-620-6

Medicine for the Soul
The Complete Book of Shamanic Healing
Ross Heaven
All you will ever need to know about shamanic healing and how to
become your own shaman...
Paperback: 978-1-78099-419-2 ebook: 978-1-78099-420-8

Shaman Pathways – The Druid Shaman
Exploring the Celtic Otherworld
Danu Forest
A practical guide to Celtic shamanism with exercises and
techniques as well as traditional lore for exploring the Celtic
Otherworld.
Paperback: 978-1-78099-615-8 ebook: 978-1-78099-616-5

Traditional Witchcraft for the Woods and Forests
A Witch's Guide to the Woodland with Guided Meditations and
Pathworking
Mélusine Draco
A Witch's guide to walking alone in the woods, with guided
meditations and pathworking.
Paperback: 978-1-84694-803-9 ebook: 978-1-84694-804-6

Wild Earth, Wild Soul
A Manual for an Ecstatic Culture
Bill Pfeiffer
Imagine a nature-based culture so alive and so connected,
spreading like wildfire. This book is the first flame...
Paperback: 978-1-78099-187-0 ebook: 978-1-78099-188-7

Naming the Goddess
Trevor Greenfield
Naming the Goddess is written by over eighty adherents and scholars of Goddess and Goddess Spirituality.
Paperback: 978-1-78279-476-9 ebook: 978-1-78279-475-2

Shapeshifting into Higher Consciousness
Heal and Transform Yourself and Our World with Ancient Shamanic and Modern Methods
Llyn Roberts
Ancient and modern methods that you can use every day to transform yourself and make a positive difference in the world.
Paperback: 978-1-84694-843-5 ebook: 978-1-84694-844-2

Readers of ebooks can buy or view any of these bestsellers by clicking on the live link in the title. Most titles are published in paperback and as an ebook. Paperbacks are available in traditional bookshops. Both print and ebook formats are available online.

Find more titles and sign up to our readers' newsletter at
http://www.johnhuntpublishing.com/paganism
Follow us on Facebook at https://www.facebook.com/MoonBooks
and Twitter at https://twitter.com/MoonBooksJHP